THE WILL OF DIVINE LOVE

ALSO BY KESS FREY

Human Ground, Spiritual Ground
Paradise Lost and Found
A Reflection on Centering Prayer's Conceptual Background (2012)

Centering Prayer and Rebirth in Christ on the Tree of Life
The Process of Inner Transformation (2013)

The One Who Loves Us
Centering Prayer and Evolving Consciousness (2014)

THE WILL OF DIVINE LOVE

Centering Prayer
and Spiritual Psychology

KESS FREY

Lindisfarne Books | 2016

2016
Lindisfarne Books
An imprint of Anthroposophic Press / SteinerBooks
610 Main St., Great Barrington, MA
www.steinerbooks.org

❊

ABOUT THE COVER IMAGE: Sacred Heart of Jesus
Christ overlooking and interpenetrating the drama
and game of God's Great Adventure on Earth; with
masks of Comedy and Tragedy below and stars of
space (other worlds) in the background. The masks of
Comedy and Tragedy represent duality and the pairs of
opposites ("on Earth"); while the Sacred Heart above
and within created reality represents non-duality and
Divine Love ("...as it is in Heaven...").

COVER AND BOOK DESIGN: Jens Jensen
COVER IMAGE: Sacred Heart stained glass, detail
(All Saints Catholic Church, St. Peters, MO);
starry background NASA, ESA, Hubble, HPOW;
"Blue Marble" from Apollo 17 (courtesy
NASA Johnson Space Center).

LIBRARY OF CONGRESS CONTROL NUMBER: 2016930434

ISBN: 978-1-58420-995-9 (paperback)
ISBN: 978-1-58420-996-6 (eBook)

Contents

This book is dedicated to the memories of Paul Ilecki, Pete Kimack, Blaine Shaw, and Michael Shorb—artistic friends who, each in his own way, enriched my life and fully embraced the drama and game of God's Great Adventure. May their souls be well rested in God and the Will of Divine Love!

ACKNOWLEDGMENTS

I am especially grateful for the inner guidance and inspirations of the Spirit that have allowed me to write this book. Centering Prayer practice and the teaching of Thomas Keating are fundamental to what I'm able to do as a writer.

As the Will of Divine Love allows for both Comedy and Tragedy in our lives, I am grateful to Pete Kimack and Blaine Shaw, who, years ago through their art, their lives, their examples, and their wisdom, taught me about the depths and the heights of the human condition and its possibilities—from "skid row" to "galaxy pop!" I am grateful to the late Paul Ilecki, who introduced me to his "Just Noticing" practice; and to Michael Shorb, whom I met years ago at UC Irvine, and who taught me about poetry, literature, and mythology.

I'm very thankful to Ed Guancial of Contemplative Outreach in Dallas, Texas, for his help with the diagrams of "Tielhard de Chardin's Curve of Evolution" (page 45) and "Spiritual Psychology in God's Great Adventure" (page 112); to Carl Arico for his kind support and foreword; and to Jens Jensen for his good work on the cover image and layout of the text.

May the inner wealth of our divine inheritance be discovered and enjoyed by every living soul journeying through the drama and game of God's Great Adventure!

FOREWORD

FR. CARL J. ARICO

Once again, Kess Frey has ventured into new applications to the world view of the spiritual life and, in particular, into how centering prayer plays an important role in this new but ancient journey.

He has a vision so expansive that it requires numerous voyages for those who truly wish to explore the spiritual journey with new eyes and new ears. I found that reading the texts out loud in a *lectio divina* format deepens the experience.

Imagine seeing God's Great Adventure from three different perspectives: created reality through the view of the Tree of Life; created reality through evolving consciousness; and above all in my view, through the mind and heart of the "cosmic scout/guide" Tielhard de Chardin's "Curve of Evolution." The image of God comes alive in so many different ways—duality has seen its day—we are in the era of non-duality—in the oneness of it all.

Over and above what I've already mentioned, I was especially moved by three chapters:

Chapter 5, "Centering Prayer and Spiritual Psychology." The distinction between the Macro-spirituality of God, and the micro-spirituality of creatures, all rooted in psychology, which is "the handmaid of spirituality." In Spiritual Psychology (Transpersonal Psychology), the personality is meant to become an instrument for the expression of our deep inner self or spiritual nature in the service of the Will of Divine Love. Centering Prayer—a prayer of consent—is a key and a map into this expression and service of the Will of Divine Love. The prayer gently breaks thru the Three Walls of Meditation—the Wall of

Thoughts, the Wall of Energy, and the Wall of Silence. Kess applies the insights of the three chapters dealing with God's Great Adventure to exploring this topic.

Chapter 7: "Working with the Unconscious: Seven Psycho-spiritual Practices." I am very familiar with and celebrate four of the practices: using an Active Prayer Sentence, the Way of the Cross, the Welcoming Prayer, and the Forgiveness Prayer. But I was enlightened by his insights into working with dreams, the creative arts, and the "Just Noticing" practice. This chapter is a marvelous example of how Kess is building and expanding on the teaching and wisdom of Fr. Thomas Keating and Contemplative Outreach.

Chapter 9," The Will of Divine Love." Let me quote the opening paragraph:

> The will of Divine Love is simple: We are utterly loved by God. God is within all of us and, with tender care and longing, God wants us to know God's presence and love deep in our hearts. This simple realization is the most wonderful discovery that holds the potential to free us from fear, sorrow, loneliness, and suffering—if we can integrate its implications and meaning into our consciousness and live true to it in human ground. Divine Love calls us to live free into the light of God's presence and love within us. I was briefly shown this sacred truth many years ago, in my mid-twenties, when something extraordinary happened that greatly enriched my life.

I end the quote there and invite you to experience on your own the details of the journey of a soul.

In conclusion, through the years I have found it worthwhile to see the spiritual journey/life through many different eyes, but I have become more convinced than ever it is all about Love—Divine Love is the essential element that gives meaning to all the theories and all the approaches. I recall the question asked of Jesus, what was the most important and greatest commandment (Matt. 22:36–40).

Or as Kess expresses so well at the end of his book,

As Love determines Justice, so does Will determine Destiny. We come from Divine Love and our destiny, as individual souls, is to consciously evolve into and become the Divine Love that we, in truth, already are. We have but to grow in and choose love, and to unite our will to that of Divine Love.

Fr. Carl J. Arico
December 5, 2015

PREFACE

"*As love determines justice, so does will determine destiny.*"
This ancient aphorism, received intuitively years ago from an old soul or "Master of Compassion," expresses the eternal basis of Cosmic Spiritual Law and central theme of this book. It tells us that the Will of Divine Love is the secret motivating impetus and inspiration of created reality. I've meditated and reflected on the psycho-spiritual and existential implications of this profound aphorism for many years, in relation to psychological wellbeing, life's meaning, and the biblical wisdom teaching: *God is love...and whoever remains in love remains in God and God in him* (1 John: 4:16). The three simple words, "God is love," are perhaps the greatest clue we have to the mystery of God or non-created Reality; and Genesis 1:26–27 (which tells us humans are created in the divine image and likeness) is probably our greatest clue to the mystery of each individual soul's salvation and Original Goodness.

This book explores and expresses some of the salient implications of the above revealed truths in relation to Centering Prayer and God's Great Adventure in created reality, which is acted out and unfolding in the life of each soul created in the divine image. Additionally, the book aims to vision real possibilities for our individual and collective spiritual growth and consciousness evolution by offering some theoretical and practical guidelines in understanding and action for the implementation of the divine plan to complete and perfect God's creation within and among us.

The divine presence is ubiquitous throughout created reality, but in ways that are normally hidden from the sight of our conscious awareness. The Unconscious, as a living, functioning reality of Spirit and soul, is the great discovery of Modern Psychology. This discovery, combined with the notion of consciousness evolving from human stages into the divine, has brought science and spirituality together, opening up a new perspective for relating to God, religious truths, and the mysteries of existence. This unfolding vision, expressed by new concepts in fresh language, is consistent with the mystical insights and meanings to be found in all the world's authentic religious, contemplative, and spiritual traditions, East and West. The chief obstacles to fulfilling humanity's spiritual potential lie in the unconscious entrenchment of the false-self system and its emotional happiness programs in soul and society. Centering Prayer and other psycho-spiritual practices address this challenge head-on; for as our motivation and consciousness change, so does the world we live in change.

GOD'S GREAT ADVENTURE, PART ONE

CREATED REALITY AND THE TREE OF LIFE

I

The Ultimate Mystery—called by many names in many tongues—is non-created Reality. It is the one divine source, sustainer, and primal mover of all existing in the great energy field of created reality. Non-created Reality, commonly referred to as "God," is the timeless, unimaginable perfection of infinite, self-abiding love, truth, and freedom transcending the greatest possible imaginings of our highest ideals. Hence, it is Ultimate Mystery and Ultimate Reality manifesting *all* possibilities in the Great Adventure of its Self-expression, which is God's creation in time and space.

God's creation is God's Great Adventure. As God's spiritual children created in the divine image (Gen. 1:27), we are each an important part of God's Great Adventure. Each of us is an individual microcosm of the universal Macrocosm, an explorer of experience, an actor on the stage, a vital part of life's unfolding drama centered in the heart of God. The Divine Consciousness is living it all through us, with us and in us; and through every creature and evolving consciousness in created reality. This entire ongoing process is governed perfectly by the Will of Divine Love, which supplies the boundless energy, creating the organizing Laws of limitation and infinite expanse and setting the righteous rules for the incredible drama and game of God's Great Adventure manifesting everywhere and in each individual soul.

This is the adventure of God becoming not-God, of the limitless becoming limited, and the perfect becoming imperfect, so that it may—through its creation of countless microcosmic souls—evolve their individual consciousness up into a newer and seemingly greater (i.e., numerically larger) perfection. This Divine Mystery of reality and illusion, of *is* and *is not*, allows for *all* possibilities, is riddled with paradox in the dance and contradictions of opposites, and may not be fully grasped by any of our created points of view. Otherwise, it would not be the Ultimate Mystery. At most, we may be graced to intuit intimations and insights of God's fathomless mystery and abiding presence within and among us. The key to this mystery is Divine Love; for all of created reality, together with the physical and spiritual Laws governing it, is the ongoing manifestation of the Will of Divine Love.

Each individual soul has a vested share and central place in the drama and game of God's Great Adventure through the choices of our individual free will and the consequences of those choices. A unique version of God's Great Adventure is being played out in the life and experience of each of us. The full dramatic potential of God's creation is held within each unique soul created in the divine image. How the story unfolds for each of us is relative to our choices and circum-stances, to our awareness and our options.

Just as each individual's will is our instrument for the exercise of whatever personal freedom we may have, so is the Will of Divine Love the means for the exercise of God's infinite Freedom. This is so because "God is love" (1 John 4:8). The mystery of love in its fullness is the Macro-Mystery of God, and, God being Spirit, Divine Love is the key and foundation of creation's Spiritual Psychology, which is the inner psycho-spiritual working basis motivating each soul and all of created reality. This is the first principle of Spiritual Psychology wherein the Divine Love of non-created Reality *is* the basis of creation within the absolute consciousness of God. Everything happening and existing in created reality is contained, supported, and embraced in God's ever-present, non-dual consciousness and Divine Love.

We experience at least faint intimations and brief insights into this timeless, omnipresent mystery whenever we are touched, moved, or inspired by love in our life. Love changes everything in an instant by transporting consciousness from the mundane to the sublime, from the human to the divine. All authentic experiences of love are experiences of God's presence and action in us and in our life, though we may not recognize them as such. This recognition or lack thereof depends on the degree of spiritual sensitivity, awareness, and maturity with which we relate to love when we encounter it.

True love brings us into a place of deep humility, preciousness, and awe, if we're not already there. When we experience the good, the true and the beautiful, we are blessed by love's presence and graced by a subtle inbreathing of divine life into our soul. Divine light, life, and love are gifts of the Spirit that lift us above the heaviness, limitations, and blinders of our creaturely human existence. These peak experiences of divine light, life, and love are priceless blessings of freedom and joy in the soul that enrich our life; serving to awaken and transform us within, and to make our life increasingly rewarding, meaningful, and worth living.

Love awakens us into the presence of the sacred within and around us, allowing us to share in the limitless wealth of heart's treasure to find—the yearning fulfillment we all long for as our souls cry out from deep inside, telling us that love's ideal freedom and fulfillment are possible for *all* of us to reach, each in our own way. Only God's holy love can complete the soul in the yearning hunger and questing journey of its seeking after freedom and fulfillment. This archetypal quest of the soul is the eternal game and ultimate drama of God's Great Adventure playing out in each of us across the sounding stretch of time in the silence of God's heart.

Thus, finding and growing in love is a matter of ultimate concern for each of us, if we understand our true spiritual needs. Each soul's lasting happiness and greatest fulfillment lie in its capacity to evolve into growing harmony with the Will of Divine Love. The Will of Divine Love is the basis of created reality and all Laws governing it, including the physical. Hence, as Francis Bacon (AD 1561–1626) famously wrote, "Nature may be commanded only by being obeyed." This is a statement of profound wisdom and insight applying to all the Laws of created reality, whether physical or spiritual. The Laws of created reality are expressions of the Will of Divine Love. Our soul's deepest need and greatest fulfillment lie in the conforming of our individual will to the universal Will of Divine Love. This basic principal of Spiritual Psychology has far-reaching implications and is well worth meditating upon.

II

Why did the One Who loves us choose to embark upon God's Great Adventure? Why did God choose to create? Three plausible answers have been given to this primal existential question: 1) to dream and play for fun and drama within the Divine Consciousness in order to manifest *all* possibilities of what may be created and experienced; 2) to experience what it'd be like to be not-God, which is what happens when God, the Great Cosmic Dreamer of created reality, forgets in us that the play is actually a dream so that the divine consciousness of non-created Reality is temporarily lost or forgotten as the drama, play, and dream of creation become our only known reality; and most important, 3) to share God's overflowing Divine Love and goodness with all souls existing in created reality. These are three plausible answers to why we exist and why God continues creating within the divine consciousness.

Sharing in God's love is the higher purpose of our soul's spiritual journey and consciousness evolution. However, the fulfillment of this higher purpose does not seem to be an automatic outcome of our creation as individual souls. Spiritual growth, our growth in love, requires our freely chosen consent, willing participation, effort, and cooperation with God's plan for us under the Will of Divine Love. Love gives us liberty to choose. This is a second fundamental principle of Spiritual Psychology. Just as God apparently chose to create us and the multidimensional happening universe of what is, so are we given the opportunity to say "yes" or "no" to God's plan for us—assuming we are educated enough to realize that there is such a plan and that we have this choice. It's the Will of Divine Love for us to have free will, especially the freedom of this most basic existential question, "to be or not to be."[1]

Our freedom and ability to say "yes" or "no" to God's plan for us as individual evolving souls is an essential part of the drama and game of God's Great Adventure. God has given us a measure of free will by giving us the need to make choices in the living of our lives. On the spiritual level, we have to choose among various attitudes and moral/ethical alternatives. This element of liberty, which often finds us attracted in contrary directions, serves to make the game and drama of human life more challenging, interesting, and somewhat unpredictable.

We can never know for certain what someone else, or our own unconscious, is going to do. The moral/ethical dimension of human free will has traditionally been referred to as the archetypal conflict between "Good and Evil," "creation and destruction," "to be or not to be." Good and Evil, which may be defined in various ways, are two basic opposing spiritual principles in human nature and created reality. We shall discuss this important topic in Spiritual Psychology and God's Great Adventure in detail in chapter 4. First, we need to touch upon the origins of created reality, individual souls, and the evolution of our consciousness from human ground into spiritual ground as intended by the Will of Divine Love.

III

Does God's Great Adventure have a pattern or design? There's obviously some organization of "intelligent design" to the way things work in created reality. A diverse variety of models and theories as to what Nature's creative design is have been given in the fields of philosophy, science and religion, psychology, metaphysics, and mysticism. All of these are of value and have something to teach us. There are specific models and maps of particular areas of created reality; and there are comprehensive models and maps that seek to integrate the diverse parts of creation into a unified whole (Ken Wilber's Integral Theory of consciousness evolution and the Qabalistic Tree of Life, an ancient map of consciousness in the esoteric Judeo-Christian tradition, are important examples).[2] We will look at both of these; first the Tree of Life.

The Qabalistic Tree of Life (see diagram on p. 7) offers the mind's eye a new visual field for picturing the soul and its mechanisms in relation to Christ within us. It is a detailed and nuanced map of God's Great Adventure and the inner terrain of Spiritual Psychology. This map begins at the top of the Tree in the Limitless Light of non-created Reality, with the divine choice to create within the Divine Consciousness and enter manifestation under limiting circumstances (i.e., God's choice to begin the Great Adventure and become not-God). It proceeds from there into a process of progressive unfolding to produce God's Self-expression or great work of art, which is the Tree itself and God's Great Adventure. Throughout this book, we shall use an abbreviated, simplified version of the Tree of Life to serve as a visual aid for imagining the ongoing process of God's Great Adventure, the inner terrain of Spiritual Psychology, and God's work in the soul.[3]

The Tree of Life—manifesting within the non-dual Limitless Light and eternal Divine Consciousness of non-created Reality—is made up of ten universal holy Spheres and an invisible, hidden Sphere that are the emanations and Spheres of activity of the Divine Consciousness within the Divine Consciousness. The visible Spheres consist of three Triads or groups of three Spheres descending from the top of the Tree, plus a final, tenth Sphere at the bottom. The Tenth Sphere, called "Kingdom," is the expanding physical Universe and precious human body through which we experience our life in this world.

Each Sphere on the Tree of Life is a vast domain or universe of created reality containing within it a smaller Tree. Each holy Sphere houses a variety of realms with innumerable conscious beings generally evolving up the Tree into increasing levels of spiritual awareness and activity in service to the divine plan (exceptions apart). The Tree is also made up of three vertical Pillars, called "The Pillar of Severity" on the viewer's left, "The Middle Pillar," and "The Pillar of Mercy" on the right. The Middle Pillar has four holy Spheres, and the side Pillars have three each. The Middle Pillar corresponds to the spinal column and brain in the human body while the side Pillars correspond to the two sides of the head and the torso.

The three Spheres at the top of the Tree make up the Supernal Triad of ubiquitous universal consciousnesses. These three Spheres are called "Crown," "Wisdom," and "Understanding." Crown is the all-inclusive, non-dual (without-an-opposite) consciousness of absolute

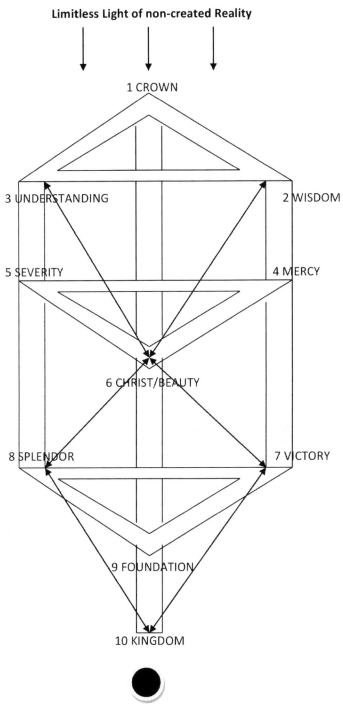

Limitless Light of non-created Reality

1 CROWN

3 UNDERSTANDING

2 WISDOM

5 SEVERITY

4 MERCY

6 CHRIST/BEAUTY

8 SPLENDOR

7 VICTORY

9 FOUNDATION

10 KINGDOM

Dark Sphere of the Abyss

Basic Tree of Life Pattern

oneness encompassing the entire Tree and integrating all of created reality. It's the place of "unapproachable light" (1 Tim. 6:16), where "the beginning of the whirling" of creation's energy originates to flow down the Tree, cascading below into the other nine holy Spheres and then, as individual souls, evolving back up again to fulfill the divine plan of God's Great Adventure. This whirling is the circular motion of various energy patterns on all levels of created reality, ranging from the largest to the smallest (from the great turning galaxies of stars down to the tiniest elementary particles in the Zero Point Field), from the physical to the spiritual (from physics to metaphysics), and from unconsciousness through the stages of evolving consciousness and love into the inconceivable Divine Consciousness and Pure Love of non-created Reality.[4] The energy of creation unfolds and evolves into new modes of expression as it moves down and back up the Tree through the ten holy Spheres.

So, the Crown Sphere at the top of the Tree and apex of its Supernal Triad initiates the process of creation on the great Tree of Life, and in each individual soul (which is a microcosmic replica of the Macrocosmic Tree—i.e., "created in God's image"). Wisdom and Understanding, forming the horizontal base of the Supernal Triad, are creation's positive and negative polar opposites or Divine Masculine and Feminine Principles, personified as "Divine Cosmic Father" and "Divine Cosmic Mother." Divine Cosmic Father and Divine Cosmic Mother generate creation, giving image, movement, form, and birth to all manifestations and pairs of opposites in created reality, including our individual souls. Their timeless ongoing blissful union generates the divine Word or only Son of God, Christ/Beauty on the Central Pillar in the Spiritual/Moral Triad immediately below the Supernal Triad. It is in and through the Word or Son (Beauty) that God's creation is manifested from the within into what we perceive as the without. This central Sphere on the Tree is present throughout creation and especially in the true integral center of each soul. All possibilities of created reality manifest through God's Word or Son Who is "the light of all people...which enlightens everyone" (John 1:1–9), in accord with the Will of Divine Love.

The divine qualities and powers of the three holy Spheres in the Supernal Triad are poured down into God's Son or Word (Christ) in the Sphere of Beauty at the bottom of the Tree's second Triad, the Spiritual Moral/Triad. The other two holy Spheres in the Spiritual/Moral Triad also pour their qualities down into God's Son, the Christ, in the Sphere of Beauty (which holds the divine image). They are called "Mercy" and "Severity" respectively, and form another archetypal pair of opposites or complementary spiritual principles in the scheme of God's divine plan. Thus, receiving the qualities, virtues, and consciousness of all the holy Spheres above it on the Tree, the Word or Son of God (Christ) holds and integrates all the wealth and power of the first five holy Spheres on the Tree of Life, which flow into it through the energy paths connecting them (see the diagram on page 7).

It is the Divine Cosmic Mother, the Sphere of Understanding at the bottom-left of the Supernal Triad, Who gives birth to each individual soul born into God's Great Adventure on the universal Tree of Life. Following its birth, the individual soul journeys across the Great Abyss separating the Supernal from the Spiritual/Moral Triad and enters the Sphere of Mercy at the top of the Spiritual/Moral Triad. This is the holy Sphere of universal love, forgiveness, oneness, and compassion for all, where the infant soul experiences deep peace, rest, and security in a timeless nurturing atmosphere of harmony, love, and ideal contentment. During its time in the Mercy Sphere, the infant soul receives the blissful imprints of its first Paradise where conflict and disharmony are unknown. The memory of this heavenly experience remains deep in the soul's core and serves as a basis of both its inclination toward loving kindness and its spiritual "homing instinct," our deep, innermost longing to return to the peace, happiness, and wholeness of our true spiritual home in God's Love.

At some point, the infant soul immersed in the unitive harmony, intimacy, and bliss of the Mercy Sphere is transferred across the energy path leading from the Sphere of Mercy into its polar opposite on the other side of the Tree. This is the dualistic Sphere of Severity and Cosmic Spiritual Law (Justice), where the soul loses the unitive peace and security of the Mercy Sphere and meets the edgy resistance of conflicting opposites, such as Good versus Evil. The shocking pain of this sudden loss and jarring experience inflicts the Primal Wound of Separation that ends the infant soul's unknowing innocence of naïve fusion and identity with its surroundings. The Sphere of Severity gives rise to the primal sense of separation and awakens the soul's powers of discrimination that allow it to distinguish between the various opposites in created reality. This Sphere is the origin of the soul's innate spiritual conscience that intuitively discriminates between good and evil, knowing in advance *all* the outcomes of each choice it considers in the drama and game of life.

The conscience is an inner voice of divine wisdom and guidance God has placed in each soul as an essential part of its natural operating system in accord with the Will of Divine Love. Our conscience works in harmony with the Laws of Cosmic Justice and is the inner advocate for righteousness and our spiritual growth in relation to God. The Laws of Cosmic Justice are served by the dualistic Principle of Justice manifesting in the holy Sphere of Severity. These Laws are based on the higher Principle of Universal Love and oneness, which comes from the Mercy Sphere. The soul is destined to live under the dualistic Laws of Cosmic Justice until it transcends them by evolving into full harmony and union with the higher, non-dual Law of Universal Love as taught by Jesus: "Love your enemies" (Luke 6:27).

Thus, the soul receives the powers of mental discrimination and the imprints of Cosmic Spiritual Law in the holy Sphere of Severity. The wisdom and foresight of conscience—received in the Severity Sphere—are essential for guiding the soul's intelligent awareness and conscious moral/ethical decision-making process when it enters the drama and game of God's Great Adventure in human ground and the Kingdom Sphere at the bottom of the Tree. Before it enters the realm of physical incarnation in the Kingdom Sphere, however, the soul has to journey into the Central Sphere of Beauty at the bottom of the Spiritual/Moral Triad, and from there down through the three Spheres of the lower Personality/Astral Triad.

Beauty, the Tree's Central Sphere, is the seat of the divine indwelling or Higher Self in each soul, and of the Universal Higher Self (the great "I Am" of Christ) on the Macrocosmic Tree of created reality. In the ancient Hebrew Tradition (in which Qabalah and the Tree of Life first appeared in human ground as "the secret wisdom of Israel"), some of the original names or attributes assigned to the Beauty Sphere are *Ben*, the Son of *Ab*, the Father (the Wisdom Sphere in the Supernal Triad); *Mechhiah*, the Messiah, or "anointed one" (*Christos* in Greek), meaning "Redeemer" and "Savior," "Prince of Peace" (*Shalom*), which implies perfection and wholeness; "Mystical Redeemer;" "Image-Making Power;" "Separating Intelligence"; and "Adam," meaning generic humanity and all living things (see Gen. 3:20, where Adam "named his wife 'Eve' because she was the mother of *all* living").

It is the function of *Ben*, the Son and Word of God (Christ/Beauty), to do the Will of *Ab*, the Father (Wisdom), who holds the original pattern for the universal Divine Plan, which is the Will of Divine Love. As the Lord proclaims through the Prophet Isaiah:

> Just as from the heavens the rain and snow come down and do not return there until they have watered the earth, making it fertile and fruitful, giving seed to the one who sows and bread to the one who eats, so shall my word be that goes forth from my mouth; my word shall not return to me void, but shall do my will, achieving the end for which I sent it. (Isa. 55:10–11)

The end for which God's Word has come forth is to manifest created reality and bring it to perfection, as a divine work of art, through the consciousness evolution and spiritual awakening of countless individual souls.

The Beauty Sphere, in the Spiritual/Moral Triad, is the source of our true identity as spiritual beings created in the divine image and likeness (Gen. 1:26). When the descending soul moves from the Severity Sphere in the Spiritual/Moral Triad into the Central Sphere of Beauty, it receives the imprint of the divine image and indwelling Trinity (Father, Son, and Holy Spirit) into the deepest center of its innermost core. This imprint holds the divine plan for the soul's spiritual evolution back up the Tree as well as the master pattern for the archetypal drama and game of God's Great Adventure in which the soul will act as an essential player on the stage of human ground when it enters physical embodiment in the Kingdom Sphere at the bottom of the Tree.

All individual souls are united in the love of Christ through the Beauty Sphere deep within us. This common innermost true center is the spiritual ground of our shared divine inheritance and life in the One Who loves us. Its living reality in all of us is the inner secret of the perplexing drama and game of God's Great Adventure in which each of us, knowingly or unknowingly, is an essential player living and moving in the hidden heart of God within and among us. The soul's central Beauty Sphere is the home of heart's longing that inspires us with loving compassion (Mercy) and hunger for Justice (Severity) in this turning world of perplexing contradictions, conflicts, differences, and uncertainty.

The great mystical secret of human life in God's Great Adventure is that under the surface of our many different roles and appearances, we are all one and the same in the inner core of our true identity as spiritual beings under the Will of Divine Love. Through the Beauty Sphere of Christ's presence within us, we may identify in loving solidarity with the victories and defeats, the struggles and triumphs of all souls around us, near and far, in the drama and game of God's Great Adventure. The gift of this loving sense of communion with others— as our brothers and sisters in the Spirit—is the missing ingredient for each soul's awakening into the amazing wonder, beauty, and rich inner meaning of living life consciously as prayer (relating to God) in the drama and game of God's Great Adventure.

In truth, we are all co-participants sharing in a common reality of unity and diversity, connection, and relationship through the pre-existing intimacy of our hidden origins in the true center of our souls. This true center is the holy Sphere of Beauty within us all that holds the promise and potential of our divine inheritance as children of God created in the divine image of truth, beauty, and goodness under the Will of Divine Love. As individual souls playing different outer roles in the drama and game of God's Great Adventure, we are at once unique and universal, different and the same, in the holy Sphere of Beauty that upholds us all.

IV

Thus the Sphere of Beauty on the Middle Pillar in the center of the Tree is the soul's true spiritual center into which Centering Prayer ultimately brings us. Whereas the Middle, Spiritual/Moral Triad on the Tree is the soul's individual spiritual ground, the Personality/Astral Triad and Kingdom Sphere below it are the place of our individual human ground, where we enter most fully into the drama and game of God's Great Adventure. After receiving the imprints of the divine image and God's plan for its spiritual growth and consciousness evolution in the Beauty Sphere, the individual soul travels down into the Sphere of Victory at the top-right of the Personality/Astral Triad, where it receives the psycho-spiritual components of human nature.

As Beauty is the Sphere of the Will of Divine Love in the Spiritual/Moral Triad, Victory is the Sphere of our human free will below it in the Personality/Astral Triad. The Victory Sphere is the seat of our human emotions and desire nature, which give rise to various expressions of our personal free will and to drama in our life. Drama always involves attachment to outcomes, to what happens in the game of life. Hence, the idea of victory is generally associated with getting what we need or want—whether it is of an instinctual, social, secular, competitive, profane, or sacred nature. We feel like we've won when we get what we want.

Desire is the engine that runs our soul in human ground. It is the source of the motivational energy that moves us to action. We tend to see the world through the eyes of our issues, beliefs, and desires. In order for us to believe or desire something, it needs to be real for us, and we need to imagine it, to vision it, dream, it and picture it in our consciousness. Thus, in addition to involving the psychological functioning of our human emotions, desire nature, and individual free will, the Sphere of Victory is also the seat of our imagination or personal image-making power. This makes sense because our emotions, desires, free will, and imagination all work together to create our personal experiences of action and drama in the game of God's Great Adventure.

The Victory Sphere is at the bottom of the Pillar of Mercy on the right side of the Tree, with the Spheres of Mercy and Wisdom directly above it. Directly across from Victory at the bottom of the Pillar of Severity is the holy Sphere of Splendor on the left side of the Tree, with the Spheres of Severity and Understanding directly above it. Splendor is the complementary opposite of Victory, the Sphere of emotions. It is the Sphere of our intellect and thought processes, of logic, reasoning, and the concrete rational mind. When images charged with affect are sent from the Victory Sphere into Splendor across the energy path connecting them (see diagram on page 7), thoughts circulate around and elaborate upon our desires. This is a creative process in which the Spheres of Intellect and Emotions interact back and forth, exchanging energies and influencing each other. In fact, all the Spheres in the Personality/Astral Triad and on the Tree of Life as a whole are in continual interaction through the energy paths and lines of force connecting them. Thoughts circulate around our desires and issues of concern like planets around the sun. Of particular significance here is the root thought of our separate-self ego-identity (false self) that is formed in the intellectual Sphere of Splendor.

Splendor is the Sphere in which intellect conceives ego, and our human ego begins to reflect itself to itself as a separate self, apart from others and the world around us. We need the human ego as an instrument for functioning in the dualistic world of the Kingdom Sphere and human ground. Splendor is the Sphere of the legendary Lucifer (light-bearer) and his rebellious dark angels who fell from Heaven because of the sin (error) of egotistical pride and the vain ambition to rival God, the Creator (see Isa. 14:12–15). Over-identification with the intellect and separate-self sense of human ego is the pitfall of Splendor (symbolized in the story of Lucifer) to which we may be tempted when we discover the powers of intellect and succumb to the illusion of pride by misidentifying our separate-self sense as our God or true self. This "sin of Lucifer" amounts to denying the true non-created God and worshipping one's false, "homemade self" instead.

The human intellect (Splendor) is not our true identity but a limited instrument or tool intended for our right use in dealing with the questions and challenges we face in human life. It's more of a means to an end than an end in itself. To avoid getting stuck in mechanical ruts of repetition, and to think creatively, the intellect (which is essentially a processing, organizing, copying, and reasoning instrument) needs to be "impregnated" or inspired by intuitions coming from the Spheres around it. It's when the Splendor Sphere receives higher inspirations from the Spheres of the Spiritual/Moral Triad above it that intellect's true splendor may awaken and shine!

"Foundation" is the name of the third Sphere in the Personality/ Astral Triad. It's located on the Middle Pillar at the bottom of the Personality/Astral Triad directly below Beauty in the Spiritual/Moral Triad and just above the Kingdom Sphere at the bottom of the Tree. As its name suggests, Foundation is the practical basis and support of all functioning patterns and structures in the soul and created reality. It has a variety of functions and attributions, such as: memory; the automatic consciousness that reproduces all habit patterns; the animal soul of instinctual drives and passions—for food, sex, and power; telepathic connections among all life forms (including humans); sub-consciousness; primitive religious beliefs and practices; the Underworld; and the Individual and Collective Unconscious of Jungian Psychology. Foundation is fundamental to everything existing in created reality.

All forms are said to take shape in the "astral matter" of the Foundation Sphere before they "out-manifest" in human behavior and the Kingdom Sphere of physical creation at the bottom of the Tree.[5] Foundation is a kind of testing or proving ground for possibilities in the soul. All forms created there do not actually come forth into outer expression; only some of them do. When changes and new growth occur in the human personality, these are always preceded by corresponding changes in the underlying patterns of the Foundation Sphere. The Foundation Sphere and its patterns may be directly influenced by input from the other two Spheres in the Personality/Astral Triad (Victory and Splendor); by input from the Kingdom Sphere below it; and by the inner action of the divine indwelling or Christ (the Beauty Sphere) above it, which, when conditions are right, may come down into the Foundation Sphere via the Middle-Pillar energy path connecting them. This is a key to the divine action in the soul.

Before Beauty can access Foundation, there needs to be inner peace with absolute calm in the animal soul area of Foundation, plus consent of the individual will to the divine presence and action within— as happens in Centering Prayer and the gift of silent contemplation, which is an intimate activity of the Will of Divine Love. When, with our willing consent and cooperation, the divine action of Christ/ Beauty accesses the personality's underlying patterns in the unconscious Sphere of Foundation, inner purification, healing, and transformation take place over time in the soul via the unloading of toxic unconscious contents and the creation of new personality patterns grounded in the spiritual values of the Higher Self (Christ/Beauty). This is the basic inner work of Centering Prayer or "prayer in secret" (Matt. 6:6), which typically occurs outside the conscious awareness of the person who is doing the praying as he or she willingly consents to the divine presence and action within.[6]

V

Below the Foundation Sphere and the Personality/Astral Triad is the Kingdom Sphere of physical reality with which we are most familiar. This is the Sphere of the physical human body, environment, human relationships, and the vast physical Universe that we experience through our physical senses. The observation, study, and manipulation of physical reality are the province of the physical sciences (e.g., physics, chemistry, geology, biology, and astronomy, as conceived by human scientists in the Splendor Sphere of intellect). The physical sciences and their technological applications have achieved great accomplishments on the physical level but are mostly at a loss to tell us anything about the nature and origins of the consciousness in which we experience our physical world—and which allows us to study and observe it. The miracle of consciousness is so fundamental to human life that we easily ignore and take it for granted. However, without consciousness there could be no meaningful awareness of existence, no knowing that we know, and no experience of God's

Great Adventure. Consciousness equates to life knowing that it's alive and unconsciousness is akin to death. The more conscious we are, the more fully alive we are.

God, Divine Love, is the pure, perfect and Absolute Consciousness in which God's Great Adventure is always happening. The performing stage and drama of God's Great Adventure reflect the consciousness of each individual soul and all created reality beyond the relative unconsciousness of pre-living matter, moving up through progressive stages of evolving consciousness, ultimately culminating in the full emergence of God's Divine Consciousness (Love) into created reality. As a map of consciousness, the Qabalistic Tree of Life offers a graphic representation of this evolutionary process, which begins, ends, and is rooted in the mysterious divine presence of God or non-created Reality. The Divine Consciousness of non-created Reality is the ultimate ground or context in which created reality and God's Great Adventure are happening.

Consciousness precedes creation, though our human consciousness in the Kingdom Sphere obviously arises as a consequence of terrestrial evolution within created reality. Hence, there's our relative created consciousness, which evolves, and there's the absolute non-created Divine Consciousness of God, which does not evolve; it's already perfect and complete. Our ultimate goal of spiritual growth in love is union with God's non-created Divine Consciousness and manifesting it into created reality. This is the process of universal redemption. So, the Will of Divine Love is the Will of God's non-created Divine Consciousness. God's perfect Will of Divine Love, which may never be bound by our preconceptions or prejudices, is the driving principle of creation and the universal foundation of Spiritual Psychology, which proceeds, on the Qabalistic Tree of Life, from Above in the Spiritual/Moral and Supernal Triads.

The creative process of evolving consciousness and individual souls climbing the Tree of Life reverses the pattern of the soul's descent down the Tree into human incarnation as described above. That is, the process of each soul's spiritual growth and consciousness evolution begins in the Kingdom Sphere of physical life at the bottom of the Tree and then gradually proceeds back up the Tree. This movement of the soul's spiritual growth and consciousness evolution, inspired by its innate "homing instinct," has been called "the path of return" to God, the living Source of created reality that sent us forth as seeds of its substance to blossom in the One.

2

GOD'S GREAT ADVENTURE, PART TWO

CREATED REALITY AND EVOLVING CONSCIOUSNESS

I

Another, complementary way of viewing the soul's path of return to God is in terms of the six stages of evolving consciousness identified by Ken Wilber's Integral Theory. A thorough discussion of Integral Theory, which has been evolving for several years, is beyond the scope of this book. We'll simply limit our discussion to some of its core ideas and valuable insights, including the six stages of evolving consciousness.[1] These six stages of consciousness evolution occur within created reality and correspond to the entire history of humanity on Earth. Each of us sees the world through the perspective of our current stage of evolving consciousness. As consciousness evolves, our world transforms. This is true for us individually and collectively.

Each stage of evolving consciousness creates a particular range of perspectives or outlooks on life that define a general context for interpreting, experiencing, and acting in God's Great Adventure, as we shall see. Each stage in both individuals and groups evolves out of and incorporates the preceding stage(s) into itself. Each has its inherent strengths and weaknesses, its blind spots and insights, its characteristic attitudes and values. Each stage tends to assume that its way of seeing and understanding things is right and true and that all other, unfamiliar stages are inferior or not to be trusted—with the exception of the *integral stage*, which ideally recognizes and respects the necessity and relative validity of all stages, and that endeavors to combine and integrate their good points while discarding their flaws.

The first stage of evolving consciousness is the *tribal stage,* which evolved out of an earlier archaic consciousness of the Stone Age as humans began banding together in tribal groups for mutual survival and support. Integral Theory estimates that tribal-stage consciousness began around 50,000 years ago. In terms of the Tree of Life, early humans in the tribal stage lived primarily in the vital animal-soul consciousness of the Foundation Sphere—the "trying and testing" Sphere of instinctual drives (for food, sex, and power), sub-consciousness, the historical Unconscious, memory, automatic patterns, astral matter, nature spirits, and group consciousness. The refinements of intellect (Splendor Sphere) and emotions (Victory Sphere) were as yet not clearly developed. Physical safety and survival were of paramount concern to early humans living in communion with Nature where forces beyond their control (such as unruly weather and predatory beasts) often determined their fate. Life was brief and challenging for most people. It was natural and necessary for them to band together in cooperative tribal groups. This led to the development of language and humanity's first belief systems (primitive religions) to facilitate communication and pass on important information from one generation to the next.

The creation myths, shamanic religions, and magical practices of early humans were likely inspired by curiosity, imagination, discovery, and primal fears related to survival, awareness of mortality, and life's uncertainties. As we know from developmental psychology and Thomas Keating's descriptions of the false-self system, with its childish happiness programs,[2] much of human psychology and behavior is based on the principle of compensation. Early humans in the tribal stage probably compensated for their very real fears through shamanic magical practices, sacrificial offerings, and burial rites intended to placate or win favor from the gods or Nature spirits, upon whom they depended for survival, and to insure a good afterlife for their departed loved ones. Tribal-stage religion is strongly fear-based and early tribal ideas of the gods, goddesses, or Supreme Deity were directly influenced by magical beliefs, contact with Nature, and the environmental conditions in which these people lived.

The experience and evolution of early humans over thousands of years created new patterns and developments in the primal animal soul of the Foundation Sphere of memory, which became the deepest layers of what the great Swiss psychologist Carl Jung called "the Collective Unconscious."[3] The Collective Unconscious connects all of us beyond the levels of our personal unconscious. From a developmental perspective, the tribal stage of evolving consciousness corresponds to the first seven years of life, to primitive emotions, to group identity, and to the deeper levels of the Collective Unconscious in the soul's Foundation Sphere. The tribal stage involves self-centered fusion with the immediate environment; magical thinking; creative imagination; playful fantasy; psychological dependency on external powers and authority; fears regarding reward and punishment; and a strong emotional need for acceptance and belonging to one's primary familial, social, cultural, or religious group(s).

Aboriginal tribal consciousness is the historical ground from which our contemporary sense of community and group identity has evolved. Group consciousness in its many forms is a manifestation of tribal consciousness to which we may all relate (e.g., our family, ethnic, racial, linguistic, socioeconomic, religious, national, political, sexual, recreational, entertainment, and age groups). We tend to identify with our groups—their attitudes, beliefs, and values—and they in turn help us to meet our needs for security/survival/safety, sensation/pleasure, affection/esteem/approval, power/control, and intimacy/belonging. Group membership offers support from others and generally requires conformity to group expectations and norms. This has evolved into various forms of the "social contract" between individuals and the group.[4]

We tend to love our groups and their members to the degree that we are intimately identified with them. In fact, important groups, such as our family of origin, are primary places where we may learn to receive and give love in human relationships. Doing so contributes greatly to our spiritual growth and serves to make us truly human. Hence, it's natural to feel a strong sense of loyalty to the groups that we rely upon and care about. If our group is maligned, threatened, or attacked in any way, we'll probably want to defend it, if we can.

This simple fact and the pervasive reality of conflicts among various groups of humans, point to the origins of the second stage of evolving consciousness identified by Integral Theory as the *warrior stage*. Warrior consciousness exaggerates our basic instinctual need for power/control and appeared around 10,000 years ago as populations increased and neighboring tribes, competing for territory and dominance, began to violently prey upon one another.

II

From its primal origins, tribal consciousness evolved from prehistory down into today's recorded history. As populations proliferated and evolved, tribal groups and consciousness have done likewise to the point where we take the presence and power of group consciousness so for granted that we scarcely notice it as a dominating influence in our lives. We belong to our groups and our groups belong to us, or at least we think they do. As we conform to group expectations and demands—which often include defending the group, accepting its attitudes, beliefs, and prejudices, and promoting its agenda—the group gives us acceptance and support as per the "social contract."

Warrior consciousness evolved from tribal consciousness and gave it a new orientation—that of a warrior's drive to conquer and dominate others for status and gain, and to protect and defend one's own. Whereas an estimated five percent of today's world population are said to live primarily in tribal-stage consciousness (aboriginal societies), it's estimated that around twenty percent of humans are currently grounded in warrior consciousness—while we are all influenced by it to one degree of another. This may be seen by reflecting on our natural proclivity for competitions, fights, and rivalries (friendly and unfriendly); in games of sport and chance; two world wars in the twentieth century; violent revolutions and dictatorships throughout history; and the disparate, ongoing social, political, economic, sexual, religious intergroup conflicts, brutality, terrorism, and various tragic tribal wars of multigenerational hatred raging in the world today.

Slavery, the oppression of women and children, "bully religion," relentless quests for domination and financial gain in all types of competitions, situations, and relationships, and the false belief that "might makes right" are typical hallmarks of unmitigated warrior consciousness—often rationalized, justified, glorified, and supported in today's world by patriotic fervor, religious fanaticism, scientific materialism, and the amoral Darwinian doctrine of "survival of the fittest" as Nature's impersonal Law. In its darker, pathological aspects, warrior consciousness works knowingly or unknowingly in alliance with the principle of Evil to create hell on Earth in the drama and game of God's Great Adventure.

The anger, aggression, hatred, and violence of pathological warrior consciousness are obviously terribly dangerous and destructive to human civilization, but this same savage energy may also be highly useful, constructive, and creative when consciously controlled and channeled in the right directions. For example, the anger and aggression of warrior consciousness may be used positively when turned against self-destructive habits, for defending the innocent, combating corruption, and defending truth, justice, righteousness, and virtue in our self and society. It may be used for self-discipline in constructive work that needs to be done (physically and spiritually). The energy of warrior consciousness may support healthy self-restraint in resisting temptations and for self-affirmation in pursuing positive spiritual practices to overcome—with God's help—self-defeating habits of thought, feeling, and action (false-self happiness programs) that are not in the interest of our human and spiritual growth.

Additionally, physical activities and friendly games of competition—in which the players are not obsessed with winning at all costs—may involve expressions of warrior consciousness that entertain and serve as healthy, enjoyable outlets for pent-up passion and aggression that would otherwise become harmful and destructive if not released through competitions or creative activities of play and self-expression (e.g., sexual intimacy, physical exercise, and the arts). When human passions are not sublimated through constructive self-expression in the creative and performing arts, in healthy relationships, exercise, or competitions, then emotionally charged spectator sports of group consciousness and gladiator entertainment may function as socially sanctioned expressions of the warrior impulse, and as outlets for energies of fear, anger, and aggression in our souls.

The primal precursor of warrior consciousness may be seen in the universal "fight or flight" response of living organisms to threats of physical danger, as in the "predator versus prey" survival game of God's Great Adventure. In modern human relationships, this same game is played beyond the physical level whenever one person or group aims to dominate, use, harm or exploit another in any way. Pathological warrior consciousness is driven by primal anger, greed, and fear of the "other," combined with a compulsive need for power/control in order to feel safe and secure. In the psychology of obsessive warrior consciousness, power/control is both a "top-dog" end in itself and a means to meeting distorted needs for security and esteem. On the Tree of Life, both tribal consciousness and warrior consciousness are associated with the instinctual Foundation Sphere at the bottom of the Personality/Astral Triad.

The basic mindset of warrior consciousness always needs someone or something to oppose or attack. This perspective that takes adversity for granted tends to view human relationships in a very dualistic, "either/or" way that assumes everyone is after power/control and that you'll either dominate or be dominated. Equality is not seen as a realistic option. This covert or overt battle for one-upmanship applies to relationships among both individuals and groups. A basic, pragmatic assumption of mercenary warrior consciousness is that the "other" is never to be trusted, at least not until proven trustworthy by testing, being known well, and sharing a common group identity, loyalty, or personal agenda.

Even in such cases, however, there's always an element of uncertainty, because people have free will to change their minds. We may, though, safely trust that others will always say and do whatever they believe is in their self-interest and will serve to promote their personal or group agendas. This is a basic principle of warrior-consciousness psychology as found in business, politics, duplicitous diplomacy, and egocentric agendas of all types. It's commonly rationalized as being "the way of the world" where you always need to "keep your guard up," and where love for the "other," outside of family, group, or relationship loyalty, is considered a liability or weakness, a blinding force of emotion that clouds one's judgment with naive and romantic ideals. This is especially the case from the perspectives of hardened, cynical warriors who underneath their tough exteriors are actually terribly wounded souls, too fearful to trust and risk the vulnerability of personal intimacy and honest self-disclosure. Such warrior mentality, though intellectually astute and pragmatic in worldly affairs, is a sure recipe for spiritual poverty, interpersonal isolation, loneliness, and separation from the caring heart of one's soul. A pervasive underlying mistrust and fear of others is a fatal tragic flaw of overdone warrior consciousness in the drama and game of God's Great Adventure.

III

According to Integral Theory, the *traditional stage* evolved out of the tribal and warrior stages around 5,000 years ago, incorporating them into itself. The unruly brutality and chaos of the unmitigated warrior stage run wild gave rise to an acute need for law and order, rules and regulations, and to protect the peaceful populace of growing societies from violence and abuse at the hands of savage warriors who roamed the land and seas pillaging and plundering at will. In traditional-stage societies, the tribal and warrior stages serve as a basis for group solidarity and for enforcing the laws and protecting the group from both internal and external dangers and threats. Armies and police are a basis of security and support in traditional-stage societies where "national security" becomes a top priority, sometimes—as in today's world—at the cost of personal privacy and individual liberty.

Exaggerated deference to external authority figures in traditional-stage consciousness is analogous to the reliance and dependency of young children on the authority of their parents. Hence, traditional-stage groups, societies, and religions demand conformity and obedience from their members in thought, belief, and action, in order to maintain control, preserve stability, and insure security for the society in general. Deviations from group expectations and traditional norms are generally not tolerated in traditional-stage societies, which often identify the humanly created laws and decrees of the secular state with the "divine authority" of prevailing religious beliefs and the will of their God or gods. Ancient priest-kings, the rule of Caesar in the Roman Empire, the Pope and Church authority in the Holy Roman Empire, and Sharia Law in traditional Islamic societies are some examples of this. The union of church and state, involving mutually reinforcing alliances between government and religion, has held sway in traditional-stage societies throughout the world from ancient times until relatively recently, democracy and "separation of church and state" being more *modern-stage* concepts.

The overbearing authority of church, state, or charismatic leaders driving the tribal mass-mind consciousness and warrior consciousness of nations, crowds, and mobs is a phenomenon that's come down to us through the traditional stage of evolving consciousness. This is all part of God's evolving Great Adventure as lived by the Divine Consciousness with us, in us, and through us. The political, military, and economic, the social, educational, and religious systems and institutions in diverse human societies over the past 5,000 years have created the patterns of traditional-stage consciousness alive in the world today. It's estimated that forty to fifty-five percent of the world's population are living primarily based in the traditional stage, as well as *all* of the world's major religions. That is, all the world's major religions have remained primarily grounded in traditional-stage consciousness while some of the societies in which they exist (in Europe and the United States) have evolved to the secular *modern stage*. This may explain why there's been a significant decrease of interest and involvement in traditional organized religion in most modern societies, especially among younger generations.

The basic drive of the traditional stage is to maintain stability and order by repeating the past, enforcing the rules, preserving the traditions of parents and ancestors, and finding security in the "tried and true" traditions we've learned to trust. The important rites and rituals of traditional cultures and religions, built up into archetypes of passage from one state of life into another over many generations, may invoke charismatic waves of rich psychic openings and emotional meaning in the consciousness of those who participate in them wholeheartedly with sincere faith and devotion. Hence, there tends to be a deep emotional attachment to the patterns of the past from which traditional-stage groups derive beauty, inspiration, strength, and much of their identity. Traditional-stage consciousness tends to be relatively conservative and resistant to new ideas, innovations, and change—lest it lose the precious vision and charisma of its original inspiration. This is especially true in the world's religious institutions, which make up the only educated segment of dominant leadership in twenty-first-century civilization and society that has not yet fully moved from the traditional into the *modern stage* of evolving consciousness. Traditional-stage consciousness, along with the further developed *modern stage*, correlates to the Splendor Sphere of intellect on the Tree of Life and is characterized by psycho-emotional dependency on external authorities.

Personal belief systems obviously have a direct and powerful impact on people's behavior, consciousness, and perceptions of reality. For the most part, our belief systems are learned from the society in which we grow up and with which we identify (through social, cultural, educational, and religious conditioning). Hence, there tends to be strong emotional reliance on the ideas, traditions, and relationships in which we are reared. In this regard, the traditional stage offers a shared identity and valuable benefits of stability, security, protection, and predictability in our lives—plus the energetic charisma of its rites of passage and rituals of worship. On the other hand, the traditional stage also limits us by preventing us from opening to new ideas, innovations, and creativity that go beyond the structures or "outside the box" of traditional beliefs and practices.

The traditional-stage boxes of social, cultural, and religious conditioning give us needed feelings of real or imagined security and order, a safe, familiar container in which to live our lives; but they also confine us to their limitations and prejudices. Our lives need a box or container, but not one that's too restrictive of our growth, originality, and the inspiration of fresh ideas. Those who want to venture "outside the box," those who dare to take risks, experiment, and try new things, are often reckless and viewed as rebels—like the legendary Lucifer—but in some cases they come upon new discoveries and create new inventions that advance the evolution of human knowledge, art, culture, spirituality, and consciousness.

It was just such an opening outside the box of orderly tradition and an intellectual rebellion against certain rigid, culturally conditioned beliefs that ushered in the *modern stage* of evolving consciousness in Europe around 500 years ago. This was the time of the Renaissance and Enlightenment when a dramatic flux of new energy, ideas, and approaches to pursuing knowledge and human possibilities quickened the consciousness of creative and inquisitive souls in certain gifted individuals and the educated elite in Europe and America. A revolution took off in art, science, philosophy, and religion that challenged the dominance and absolute authority of the Church. This involved a rediscovery of classical Greek art and philosophy (which greatly enriched religious art, music, and literature); a wonderful and continuing flowering of classical music, literature, poetry, and drama; radical new scientific discoveries regarding natural laws, cosmology, and the evolution of life on Earth; the Protestant Reformation; and new ideas concerning individual liberty, human rights, and democracy (versus monarchy) as a basis for political power and national governance.[5]

The modern stage of consciousness encourages people to question pre-existing traditional values, beliefs, and practices, and to think independently for themselves "outside the box." This new freedom, which can be quite exhilarating, places increased responsibility on the individual. Modern-stage consciousness stresses intellectual skepticism, humanitarian values, and the importance of scientifically proven findings as a trustworthy basis for understanding reality and developing technology. In the process of doing this, it sometimes rejects all that cannot be scientifically proven—including, in extreme cases, moral/ethical values and belief in God. Hence, modern-stage consciousness has brought us the Industrial Revolution; mercenary corporate capitalism; modern medicine; automation; electronics; mass communications media; biological warfare; nuclear weapons; environmental degradation; space travel; and personal relationships to machines, computers, and smart phones that were unimaginable two hundred years ago.

Modern-stage consciousness has had a powerful influence on how many people perceive traditional organized religion, its beliefs, practices, and interpretations of life, death, and the Scriptures. As a result of scientific discoveries, critical thinking, and modern, scholarly research, literal interpretations of the Bible and the events it describes have been questioned, rejected as unreal myths contrary to scientific evidence, and regarded as well-intended adult fairy tales with moral/ethical messages designed to support social, political, economic justice, and basic human rights. Many modern-stage individuals reject religion altogether, becoming atheists or agnostics. Others in the modern stage, who subscribe to religious beliefs, realize that the traditions of their faith need to be updated via reinterpreting, reconciling, and integrating them with the proven evidence of scientific findings regarding the nature of physical reality and the history of the Universe. Ancient biblical writers and others held now-outdated worldviews with no access to current scientific knowledge. Hence, modern-stage consciousness has created a revolution in the area of religious faith and its applications to human life, relationships, society, and God's creation. In fact, all stages of evolving consciousness significantly shape how individuals and groups interpret and relate to God, religious beliefs, and spiritual practices.[6] Each stage of evolving consciousness is a new chapter in the unfolding story of God's Great Adventure.

IV

While fifteen to thirty percent of the world's population is estimated to live in the modern stage of evolving consciousness, only five to six percent are believed to be in the *postmodern stage*, and less than one percent in the *integral stage*. This suggests that over sixty percent of people in the world are living in pre-modern stages of consciousness. The postmodern stage, which has emerged in the last 150 years or so, is a stark counterbalance to the obsessive rationality, skepticism and "scientism" of the modern stage, which often eschews subjectivity and the meanings of myth.[7] There are two complementary sides to postmodernism. The first of these carries the intellectual skepticism, and doubt of the modern stage to immoderate, nihilistic extremes by doubting, deconstructing, and negating virtually everything, including morality, ethics, religious beliefs, and the integrity of individual persons.[8] This negative postmodernism leads into existential aloneness/incompleteness, empty meaninglessness, and dreaded dark nights of the soul in which the ego itself is deconstructed.

In dramatic contrast to pessimistic negative postmodernism is a brighter, lighter side that I call "positive postmodernism." Positive postmodernism embraces ideals of peace, harmony, and equality. It honors the subjectivity of each person's inner world and supports the relative validity of all perspectives and beliefs, seeing them as equally valid and true for the individuals holding them. Positive postmodernism is egalitarian to a fault, rejecting all hierarchies and ranking of higher and lower, better and worse. Everything is regarded as relative, everyone is allowed freedom to have their own subjective truth, and all of these truths are considered to be equally true because it's simply a matter of the personal subjective feelings of the individuals who believe in them. For the sake of universal equality, no absolutes are allowed in positive postmodernism.

Positive postmodernism earnestly seeks peace, harmony, and equality for all, aiming to avoid differences that could lead to conflicts, even when this means denying or ignoring objective reality. This is its blind spot. Hence, positive postmodernism is extremely tolerant and open to all points of view—so long as the rights of everyone else are respected. In positive postmodernism, everyone needs to be free to create their own personal subjective reality and "to do their own thing." This viewpoint has lead to a variety of innovative activities and creative expressions among postmodern individuals and groups.

> I've indicated some of positive postmodernism's innovative expressions in *The One Who Loves Us*, as follows: "The utopian idealism, spirituality and creative lifestyles of positive postmodernism are beautiful and inspiring.... The positive postmodern movements emerged in America in the 1960s as a variety of countercultural trends in such areas as art, music, drama, film, literature, lifestyle, fashion, social/political action, and spirituality. These included the civil rights and anti-Viet-Nam-War movements, feminism, gay rights, environmentalism, and a nascent spiritual awakening involving psychedelic drugs; Eastern Religions (e.g., Hinduism,

Buddhism and Taoism); yoga, meditation and interest in Western mysticism and esoteric traditions (e.g., astrology, metaphysics, alchemy, magic, psychic readings and phenomena, Rosicrucian spirituality, and Qabalah). The new discipline of Transpersonal Psychology, which integrates human psychology, depth psychology, and our spiritual dimension, also emerged during this time frame.

The countercultural movement of the 1960s morphed into the New Age Movement of the 1970s, which has evolved from there into the current positive postmodernism of the twenty-first century. The positive postmodern vision is one of peace and harmony for planet Earth and all its inhabitants. The entire human race is viewed as one evolving spiritual family while protecting the physical environment and its ability to support and sustain healthy life are given highest priority. Clean water, air and pollutant-free fertile land for organic farming are valued above shortsighted commercial housing, business, and industrial developments that degrade the environment while exploiting and depleting our natural resources for the sake of corporate profits. The earth sciences, ecological research, protecting the environment, and saving endangered species of life forms are all conscious manifestations of positive postmodernism. (*The One Who Loves Us*, pp. 85–86)

The postmodern stage of evolving consciousness in its positive aspects correlates to the Victory Sphere of emotional idealism on the Tree of Life.

V

The first five stages of evolving consciousness (tribal, warrior, traditional, modern, and postmodern) may be correlated to the soul's spiritual growth and consciousness evolution as rooted or grounded in the three Spheres of the Personality/Astral Triad on the Qabalistic Tree of Life: Foundation/Instinct; Splendor/Intellect; and Victory/Emotions. The sixth *integral stage* corresponds to the Sphere of Christ/Beauty at the bottom of the Spiritual/Moral Triad. These relationships are represented in the following diagram:

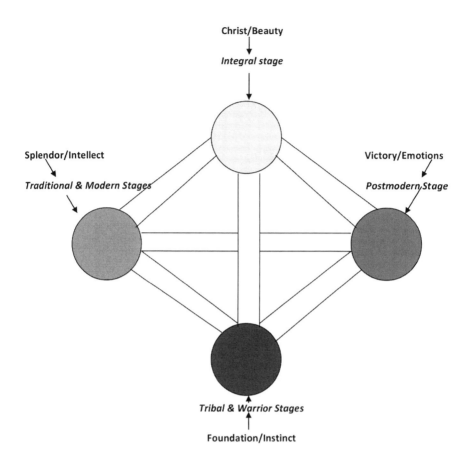

Just as each soul contains an entire Tree of Life within itself, so do we each carry all the stages of evolving consciousness within us, either as unrealized potential or as awakened actualities. The *integral stage*, corresponding to the soul's heart center and the Tree's central Beauty Sphere (Christ) in the Spiritual/Moral Triad, is where true inner wholeness and spiritual awakening become a conscious reality. Beauty, Christ the Son, is the seat of divine spirituality in the true center of each individual soul. Beauty is the Sphere of our true integral self, the Higher Self or divine indwelling. It is the origin of the divine action that purifies, heals, and integrates the soul—slowly transforming it into Christ.

As love, like an irresistible magnet, draws all things from above and below on the Tree to itself; Beauty attracts and integrates *all* the energies and dispositions of the soul's micro-spirituality: its light and dark sides, strengths and weaknesses, its flaws and perfections.[10] This harmonizing, integrating process is precisely the higher function of the *integral stage* of evolving consciousness. Christ/Beauty is the holy Sphere that creates integration and perfection in the Kingdom Sphere and in all evolving Spheres. It brings peace and harmony, divine light, love, and inspiration to life in us, as we discover these qualities through the gifts of God's grace. As Christ within us, the integral stage of evolving consciousness "separates the wheat from the weeds" (Matt. 13:24–30), eliminating what is not useful and incorporating the strengths and virtues of all stages of evolving consciousness into the dynamic wholeness of a non-dual unity that eventually fulfills the golden potential of God's divine plan and Great Adventure in individual souls.

3

GOD'S GREAT ADVENTURE, PART THREE

TIELHARD DE CHARDIN'S CURVE OF EVOLUTION

I

Divine Love embracing and transcending everything in non-dual Oneness is the paradoxical preciousness and ultimate driving force of created reality. The Will of Divine Love allows for the potential expression of *all* possibilities in the drama and game of God's Great Adventure. Each of us is a key player in this drama whether we realize it or not. We are each the leading character, star, and protagonist in our own personal version of God's Great Adventure, which hinges upon the free-will choices that God has given us, placing us in the driver's seat while God, like a hidden, backseat passenger, lives God's Great Adventure with us, in us, and through us. All souls being equally created in the divine image, we are each a precious and beloved vital center of the Great Adventure from God's omnipresent perspective, which lives and sees each of us and all creation in our uniqueness simultaneously. By giving us free will, God has given us, individually and collectively, choice and responsibility for determining how the drama and game will turn out in our innumerable unique cases. Everything is always interconnected, present, and alive within each of us, here and now.

Thus, we are co-creators with God in the drama and game of God's Great Adventure, which is an experiment of uncertain outcome that, regardless of outcomes, may ultimately end well only from the inscrutable perspective of non-created Reality, which in its limitless Self of eternal love, truth and freedom may be neither increased nor decreased by how our countless individual and collective versions of the great experiment play out. The infinite possible outcomes of God's Great Adventure, which are as many as the individual and collective groups of souls comprising the experiment, became uncertain once God took the bold step of entering into limitation; giving us basic instinctual needs, limited free will, and the need to determine our own destinies via our programmed needs, how we choose our wants, and how we use our free will in pursuing our needs and desires. It's precisely life's element of uncertainty that makes the drama and game of God's Great Adventure so interesting—especially if we can learn the game, its rules, and how to play it! The drama and game of God's Great Adventure is not only a means to an end (the fulfillment of the Divine Plan via our spiritual evolution into Divine Consciousness), but it's a meaningful, challenging, and (one hopes) enjoyable end in itself as well.

There are many individual worlds (souls) of evolving consciousness within our world here on Earth; and, beyond that, who knows how many additional worlds of evolving consciousness out there on other planets scattered throughout the vast expanding Universe of galaxies and stars spinning and turning in the Kingdom Sphere of God's Great Adventure? Each world, individual and planetary, is an experiment in the drama and game of God's Great Adventure. The cast of players in this Universe must be diverse and legion beyond our reckoning. Each player we meet is a precious expression of the Will of Divine Love.

As to the results of this grand experiment throughout the Universe (Kingdom Sphere): who knows how many planets like ours there are where the experiment of God's Great Adventure has failed because too many souls knew not themselves as spiritual beings and followed false paths of the separate-self seeking inordinate material wealth, pleasure, fame and power in blind greed, warrior consciousness, and hatred of others? And on how many planets has this Great Adventure of free-will experiment succeeded because the consciousness of evolving souls, individually and collectively, awoke into the love and oneness of soul's inner spiritual ground and divine True Self? Creation or destruction, consciousness or unconsciousness, are the two ultimate options that now lie before us on planet Earth; and we, as a species, are currently moving simultaneously toward both of them: that is, toward lack of cooperation, poisoning our planet, war and catastrophic self-destruction, on the one hand; and toward harmony with Nature, spiritual awakening, and loving cooperation, on the other.

Given the ongoing global crises now facing humanity, ranging from the physical health of planet Earth to social, political, and economic conditions, and the spiritual wellbeing of our collective and individual souls, how the intense drama of life's destiny on Earth plays out and eventually climaxes depends entirely upon the choices, behavior, and consciousness of *all* of us living on this planet. Can we awaken to the inner depth of our common spiritual core? Or will we remain lost, divided, and confused in separate-self illusions of our apparent outer differences? Which self shall we choose, to be and to do, the false or the true? Which path to pursue? "To be or not to be," as Shakespeare wrote; "that is the question?"

Could the tiny minority of human souls doing Centering Prayer and other contemplative, meditative spiritual practices, and awakening spiritually on planet Earth, somehow, by virtue of our evolving consciousness, beneficially affect the consciousness of the vast numerical majority? This is a prospect worth pondering, and it may well be a real possibility; especially since the same divine indwelling and Will of Divine Love lives in the heart of every human soul, whether known or unknown. The vision of this incredible possibility of a global spiritual awakening precipitated by a tiny minority of loving souls uniting consciously in the Will of Divine Love—which seems impossible from perspectives of practical worldly "common sense" or cynical modern-stage scientific materialism—first occurred to me as a college student many years ago, in discussion with a friend who introduced me to the book, *Man's Place in Nature*, by the now famous French Jesuit priest, paleontologist and theologian, Pierre Tielhard de Chardin.

II

Writing in the first half of the twentieth century, de Chardin was one of the first deep thinkers to express basic insights and sacred truths of mystical spirituality in modern scientific language, using concepts based on actual discoveries of scientific theory and research.[1] De Chardin's modern-stage writings were initially censured and suppressed from publication by the traditional-stage Roman Catholic Church; but, in the wake of Vatican II (after de Chardin's untimely death in 1955) his works were accepted and have since received high acclaim as a healing bridge for the bitter rift between the discoveries of secular modern science, the outdated cosmological dogmas of traditional organized religion, and the amazing insights of contemplative spirituality and mysticism.

In *Man's Place in Nature*, Tielhard de Chardin approaches evolution from the perspective of the physical sciences such as physics, chemistry, and biology, but includes the psycho-spiritual dimension of our evolving consciousness. He shows that there's a persistent pattern of growing complexity in the evolving formations of pre-living and living matter on Earth (the first two stages of evolution). The development of living matter out of pre-living matter gave rise to the Biosphere—the ecological envelope containing all organic life forms on the planet and the living web of their complex interrelations. The same principle of growing complexity that produced the Biosphere, when applied to living-matter-with-consciousness in humans, gives rise to the formation of what de Chardin calls "the Noosphere" (pronounced "*nous-sphere*"), which is the psycho-spiritual equivalent of the Biosphere. "*Nous*" is a Greek word meaning "mind" or "intellect." As de Chardin puts it: the Noosphere involves a movement toward "intensifying psychic interiority," leading to an "eventual convergence" and integration of individual centers of consciousness on a planetary scale; a dramatic collective awakening into our shared spiritual dimension. The same evolving energy that is now our consciousness was once relatively unconscious living matter and, before that, pre-living matter.

The Noosphere is an evolving ecological envelope of a non-physical, psycho-spiritual nature containing the thoughts, feelings, consciousness, and sub-consciousness (including Jung's Collective Unconscious) of all living-matter-with-consciousness on Earth—and perhaps more. The Noosphere is the psychic atmosphere of our planet, the evolving group mind or soul of humanity that may include other conscious life forms as well. It is Earth's non-physical psycho-spiritual matrix wherein whatever each of us thinks, feels, says, or does has a direct, though generally unconscious, impact and influence upon everyone else. As de Chardin points out, the implications of the Noosphere are quite astounding; since it represents a transition from the outer physical "exteriorization and expansion" of life forms on Earth into a complementary process of deepening "interiorization," a contraction of self-aware consciousness turning in on itself toward a universal all-embracing center beyond space and time that de Chardin calls "the Omega Point." This Omega Point, which is reached when a planetary Noosphere completes its evolution,[2] is identified with the Divine Consciousness of God in whose omnipresent awareness the entire drama, game, Great Adventure, and experiment of created reality is taking place. The Noosphere is a product of evolution *in* created reality that evolves as our individual and collective consciousnesses evolve. Its destination as awakening consciousness is the non-created Source of life's origins. As consciousness evolves, our world transforms again and again until Omega Point is realized.

De Chardin uses the example of a vertical curve, like that running from the South Pole to the North Pole along the Earth's outer surface, to represent the double, expanding and contracting arc of evolution on our planet. The expanding arc of evolution runs from the South Pole to the Equator of de Chardin's Curve, while the arc of contraction runs from the Equator up to the North Pole or Omega Point at the curve's summit. The South Pole represents the Alpha Point or beginning of evolution with the appearance of pre-living, inorganic matter, which evolved out of the primal energy of Earth's original molten mass that was exploded from the Sun perhaps three or four billion years ago. As the planet's surface gradually cooled down, a multitude of chemical reactions took place and eventually water appeared, covering much of the globe. This led to the requisite conditions for the second major stage in the process of evolution, the appearance of living matter (some of which may have come from extraterrestrial sources like comets carrying bacteria that collided with the Earth).[3] Owing to whatever influences, complex life forms eventually appeared on the Earth's surface. Thus began the Biosphere and evolution's lower arc of expansion, moving from the symbolic South Pole of de Chardin's evolutionary Curve toward its "Equator," which, as de Chardin points out, is the point furthest from the Earth's central axis, representing the timeless, omnipresent center of creation's origin and ending extended into three-dimensional time and space.

The upward movement of evolution's energy from the state of pre-living matter into that of living matter and toward the vertical curve's "Equator" is the period of outer expansion lasting hundreds of millions of years. During this time, the grand experiment of evolution randomly fanned out like branches growing on a tree in diverse directions—feeling its way, by trial and error, into new possibilities for organization and manifestation. Hence, creation's primal energy has manifested itself into a wide variety of interrelated pre-living and living forms, as exists today. The culmination of evolution's movement up the arc of expansion to the Equator of de Chardin's Curve was living-matter-with-consciousness in the human species to which we all belong.

Human evolution, spurred on by expanding populations and a complex socialization process, has brought us to the figurative Equator or midpoint of evolution's double arc of ascent. This equatorial midpoint correlates, in humans, to the development of our separate-self ego-identity within the dualistic ego-consciousness that has evolved up the arc of expansion along with the proliferation and evolution of diverse life forms. It is a relative, or variable, ego-consciousness that allows us and other organisms to distinguish one thing from another. This consciousness is absolutely necessary for functioning and survival in the physical world for *all* organisms that need to interact with their environments. All ego-consciousness is based on the principle of duality (separation) and always includes a perceiving subject and its object(s) of perception. In the most rudimentary forms of ego-consciousness (which belong to the Foundation Sphere on the Qabalistic Tree of Life), the perceiving subject behaves instinctively or automatically and does not perceive itself reflectively. It only perceives and responds to its object(s) of perception. De Chardin calls this initial mode of ego-consciousness "direct psychism."[4]

The instinctive ego-consciousness of "direct psychism" evolves up the arc of expansion on de Chardin's Curve and, as it moves closer to the Equator, gradually develops a capacity for self-reflection or what de Chardin calls "reflective psychism." This development in ego-consciousness correlates directly with the evolution of growing brains in various organisms, and what de Chardin calls "cerebralization."[5] The capacity of the perceiving subject in ego-consciousness to remember things consciously (as opposed to instinctively or subconsciously), and to reflect back on itself (relate to itself as an object of perception), was a major step in the process of evolving consciousness. It is this evolutionary development that gives birth to the assumption of a consciously perceived separate-self sense of ego-identity within ego-consciousness. This separate-self sense of ego-identity and "reflective psychism" reaches its zenith on the Equator of de Chardin's Curve, where it becomes most pronounced—in fact, overly exaggerated into a "false self" of absolute ego-identity. At this point, the exaggerated separate-self sense of too much ego-identity becomes dangerously problematic in self-centered human beings.

In terms of the Qabalistic Tree of Life, the evolution of conscious self-reflection and ego-identity in ego-consciousness corresponds to the movement of relative ego-consciousness from the instinctive, animal-soul Foundation Sphere in the Personality/Astral Triad up into the Triad's Splendor Sphere of intellect and objective thought processes. As mentioned earlier, Splendor is the Sphere where over-identification with intellect and ego-identity takes place. What happens in Splendor (the Sphere of "reflective psychism" on the Equator of de Chardin's Curve) is an exaggeration of the separate-self sense of ego that, in reflecting itself to itself as a separate-self, morphs into the illusion of an absolute ego-identity that perceives itself to be completely separate and apart from everything and everyone else—as opposed to relatively separate and apart. This illusory and absolute sense of ego-identity is symbolized by the character of Lucifer (light bearer), the legendary fallen angel who succumbed in his self-reflective splendor to the sin of pride and who wanted to rival the unseen God of non-created Reality, in the biblically inspired myth. This temptation and others related to it are pitfalls we all face in self-reflective consciousness in the Splendor

Sphere and on the Equator of de Chardin's Curve. A central problem of the modern human condition is that we tend to remain stuck there.

The mistaken belief in an absolute ego-identity gives rise to a multitude of serious human problems (e.g., feelings of existential aloneness/incompleteness and alienation from God); the false-self system and its misguided happiness programs; afflictive emotions; moral/ethical degradations; and failures to honor and respect the legitimate rights and needs of others when doing so interferes with our self-centered desires. The perception of one's self as an absolute ego-identity separate from and in competition with everyone else leads us astray into error and sin. It is essentially a trap of needless isolation and limitation, a pathological illusion of too much ego created by the false, spiritually ignorant assumption that the duality of mutually exclusive opposites is the ultimate basis of reality.

In truth, the non-dual oneness of Divine Love is reality's ultimate basis; and it's also our true nature as spiritual beings. Non-created Divine Love is the ever-present Source whence duality, creation, and the drama and game of God's Great Adventure originate within the Divine Consciousness. Awakening permanently into full conscious realization of this timeless truth is the ultimate goal of our spiritual growth and the evolution of human consciousness into Divine Consciousness. This spiritual awakening corresponds to the gradual movement of human consciousness from the separate-self Equator of de Chardin's Curve up through its higher arc of "contraction" and "interiorization" leading finally into the transcendent Omega Point of ultimate convergence and completion in the Will of Divine Love and non-dual oneness at the curve's zenith or North Pole.

As mentioned above, the Equator on de Chardin's Curve of evolution is the point where consciousness ("reflective psychism") reaches its furthest distance from creation's central axis of origins and endings (the furthest distance from our common spiritual center in Christ or God). Hence, human evolution and consciousness reaching the "Equator" in de Chardin's model is the point where our consciousness of absolute ego-identity, having fully realized, over-exaggerated and become lost in its individual separate-self sense, is the furthest from sensing or being aware of our inner depths, true center, and spiritual connection to the Will of Divine Love in us. Consequently, it's precisely at this point that the movement of evolution's energy on de Chardin's Curve needs to begin its second phase by transitioning from the arc of expansion into the arc of contraction and internalization by moving from psychic extraversion into a process of psychic introversion. De Chardin refers to this movement as a "centering process." It's in this centering process of "interiorization" that the Noosphere—which began evolving with the proliferation of self-reflective centers of ego-consciousness in humans—comes into play in a significant way.

III

In de Chardin's theory of the Noosphere, our self-reflecting human awareness undertakes the inner spiritual journey from the Equator of evolution's ascending curve toward its climatic Omega Point at the top of the curve. This noospheric centering process—already begun and continuing with the spiritual awakening of numerous individual souls, past, present, and to come—will eventually involve a radical spiritual awakening of humanity as a whole. It points to a meeting of human ground with spiritual ground in a new form of shared Planetary Consciousness. This, of course, assumes humanity does not destroy itself and the planet's ability to sustain healthy organic life before we're able to awaken to Omega Point and the divine presence within us all. De Chardin has estimated that the completion of humanity's consciousness evolution to Omega Point may take millions of years, or possibly a much lesser amount of time—since the spiritual laws governing this process are relatively unknown.

What may be said is that humanity's spiritual evolution is a function of the Will of Divine Love and, consequently, the more love there is among human beings, the more people evolve spiritually, the quicker our individual consciousnesses and the "planetary brain" or Noosphere will evolve toward Omega Point—the radical transformation of our present dualistic human consciousness into the non-dual oneness and universal love of Divine Consciousness. It could well be that only a tiny minority of spiritually awakened loving human souls—perhaps less than one per cent of the Earth's population—will suffice to create a magnetic drawing force of spiritual-energy waves in the upper regions of the Noosphere strong enough to inspire and lift the evolving consciousness of all willing humanity up into the awakening awareness of our pre-existing mutual love, solidarity, and unity in the divine presence within us all. Our individual and collective awakenings to de Chardin's Omega Point will eventually lead into the fulfillment of God's Divine Plan and the Will of Divine Love in us.

The gradual inner awakening of our human consciousness to Christ's presence in and among us will bring about the progressive movement of humanity's collective awareness from separate-self human ground into the communal spiritual ground of our global human family—the emergence of a new, *all-inclusive* tribal consciousness on a universal scale. It will mark the beginning of humanity's collective movement toward de Chardin's Omega Point on a conscious level where individuals will perceive one another not as isolated separate beings of ego-identity but as precious and unique members of a common spiritual body and bond who happen to be occupying different physical bodies (e.g., the "Mystical Body of Christ"). Each person will be perceived as belonging to our own divine Self.

Under the radically new circumstances of this spiritually awakened noospheric consciousness, whatever we do unto one another we shall experience directly as doing unto our self. In other words, we will know via direct perception and felt experience that we are all One in the love, truth, and freedom of our common core and Source. Under these enlightened circumstances of spiritually transformed awareness; hatred, dishonesty, and war will be out of the question, impossible to buy into or carry out! This will be the end of humanity as we now know it—conflicted and compromised by agendas of the false-self system and its emotional programs for happiness. It will initiate the graduation of our species as a whole from the limitations, blindness, and suffering of human ground into the new freedom, love, and divine light of our spiritual ground. This is ultimately what we are all praying for in seeking to serve the Will of Divine Love.

On the Qabalistic Tree of Life, this inner transformation process corresponds to the movement of individual and collective human consciousness and identity from the Personality/Astral Triad and

Kingdom Sphere, at the separate-self Equator on de Chardin's Curve, up into a deeper awakening and centering process of convergent identities in the Beauty Sphere (Christ) and Spiritual/Moral Triad as consciousness evolves toward Omega Point. The meeting of our human ground with our spiritual ground on the Tree of Life corresponds to a meeting of creation's ascending physical evolution with the higher energies and guidance of its overshadowing spiritual Source. All of this happens individually and collectively in accord with the Laws of Cosmic Justice (Severity Sphere) and is inspired from within and above by the Will of Divine Love (Mercy Sphere and Supernal Triad).

In this process, higher Spheres on the Tree of Life (e.g., in the Spiritual/Moral and Supernal Triads) make contact with lower Spheres (Personality/Astral Triad and Kingdom Sphere) to energize, guide, and inspire them, and to further the divine plan of spiritual growth and consciousness evolution in created reality. This corresponds directly to the movement of evolving consciousness on de Chardin's Curve of Evolution from its Equator Point up toward its Omega Point at the top. It also corresponds to the movement of evolving human consciousness through the tribal, warrior, traditional, modern, and postmodern stages (Personality/Astral Triad) of Integral Theory into the "integral-and-beyond" stages (Spiritual/Moral and Supernal Triads). These complementary maps of spiritual growth and evolving consciousness—that is, de Chardin's Evolutionary Curve and Theory of the Noosphere, the Qabalistic Tree of Life, and Integral Theory— all provide us with insightful ways of viewing the mysterious process of our ongoing participation in the divine plan, drama, and game of God's Great Adventure. Each of us, in our individual spiritual growth and journey, is contributing to the evolution of our planetary Noosphere and to the fulfillment of God's divine plan. Below is a diagram representing de Chardin's Curve of planetary Evolution in relation to Integral Theory's six stages of evolving consciousness. The "Extended Central Axis" in this diagram represents the omnipresent center of non-created Reality or God-Consciousness that is, to quote Augustine, *a circle whose center is everywhere and whose circumference is nowhere*:

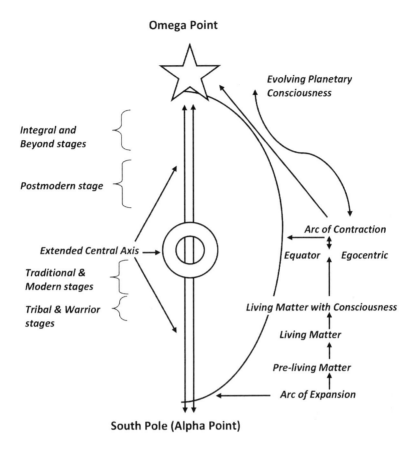

Tielhard de Chardin's Curve of Evolution

IV

A burning question crying out, consciously, or unconsciously, in the heart of each soul is: What is my life's purpose, its higher purpose? In the context of de Chardin's Noosphere, we may ask, what can I do to further the process of global consciousness evolution and spiritual awakening? How may I serve the Divine Plan and help to improve the human condition for all of us? Since the evolution of individual souls from human ground up into spiritual ground serves to promote the evolution of humanity as a whole from human ground into spiritual ground, there is perhaps no greater service any of us may give for the betterment of humanity than to undertake—in whatever ways suit us—the inner work and outer activities of our own spiritual growth and consciousness evolution. Whatever each of us thinks, feels, and does, consciously or subconsciously, and all that we desire is feeding energy into the Noosphere and thereby affecting the consciousness of everyone else on the planet. The more love and goodwill there are expressing in this world, the better off we all are. The more we allow the divine action to purify our souls and evolve our consciousness into harmony with the Will of Divine Love, the more humanity as a whole may be inspired and uplifted by our ongoing contributions to the Noosphere. We are all interconnected and united in the Noosphere's psycho-spiritual envelope of evolving consciousness.

All people who are actively doing spiritual practices like Centering Prayer and other forms of meditation, and who long for social, political, economic justice, human freedom, and peace in our world are contributing directly to the evolution of the Noosphere and the collective will toward spiritual awakening throughout humanity. This world will not change permanently for the better by outwardly persuading or forcing everyone to agree on a particular religious faith, political philosophy, or socioeconomic system. It will not improve by one group dominating another. Only by our individually and collectively awakening into divine love within us, and to the direct consciousness of our inner oneness with *all* people in love, will the world change permanently for the better. This radical awakening of humanity to our common life in the Spirit, to our life in Christ, is the essence of Tielhard de Chardin's vision of where the Noosphere is intended by God and the Will of Divine Love to take us.

In *The Future of Man*, a collection of articles written by Tielhard de Chardin between 1920 and 1955, de Chardin writes, among other things, of the Noosphere, the evolution of humanity into an "Ultra-Human," "the Phases of a Living Planet," "the End of the Species," and "the End of the World." He writes, "It is beginning to be possible to calculate in millions of years *the average life of a species*," and, "The *End of the Species* is in the marrow of our bones" (p. 301). These statements are not intended by de Chardin to foreshadow a dark and meaningless future for humanity but to herald the possibility of our transformation into a new reality of Planetary Consciousness, "a new breakthrough and a rebirth, this time outside Time and Space, through the very excess of unification and coreflexion," which characterize the maturity of a planetary Noosphere as it completes its evolution from human ground into spiritual ground and union with God. De Chardin hastens to note that what he calls "coreflexion" does not entail a diminution (as some naysayers wrongly fear) but an increase of the "person." He adds with emphasis—in moving from the perspective of ego and duality into authentic non-duality—*"union does not confound but differentiates"* (p. 303). In other words, the many are integrated into the One while remaining as many in their individuality and uniqueness. Nothing of value is ever lost while more than we may imagine of wonder and goodness is gained in the fulfillment of our destiny as spiritual beings under the perfect Will of Divine Love. This is simply a matter of faith and trust in the goodness of God in the face of our human uncertainty, doubt, fear, and ignorance. As Thomas Keating has said, "Guarantees are for people of weak faith."

What Tielhard de Chardin has expressed in scientific language he has also stated in spiritual or religious language. For example, he equates "Noogenesis" (the completion of a Noosphere's evolution) with "Christogenesis" and the theology of Paul: "At that moment, St. Paul tells us (1 Cor. 15, 23ff) when Christ has emptied all created forces (rejecting in them everything that is a factor of dissociation and superanimating all that is a force of unity), he will consummate universal unification by giving himself, in his complete and adult Body, with a finally satisfied capacity for union, to the embrace of the Godhead" (*The Future of* Man, p. 310). In mentioning Christ's "complete and adult Body," de Chardin is referring to the idea or fact:

And since Christ was born, and ceased to grow, and died, *everything has continued in motion because he has not yet attained the fullness of his form.* He has not yet gathered about Him the last folds of the garment of flesh and love woven for him by his faithful. *The mystical Christ has not reached the peak of his growth* ... and it is in the continuation of this engendering that there lies the ultimate driving force behind all created activity ... Christ is the term *of even the natural* evolution of living beings. (*The Future of Man,* p. 307)

Our spiritual growth in love, through Centering Prayer and other spiritual practices, contributes directly to the evolution of our planetary Noosphere *and* to the growth of the Mystical Body of Christ. These two are, in fact, one and the same. In Tielhard de Chardin's vision, as human consciousness evolves into divine consciousness, all the creative energy comprising pre-living matter, living matter (the Biosphere) and living-matter-with-consciousness (the Noosphere) will ultimately (perhaps in millions of years or much less time) dematerialize planet Earth and transform it (us) into a star of pure consciousness and divine love beyond time and space. This is Tielhard de Chardin's inspired vision of Christ's Second Coming, the end of the world as we now know it, and the establishment of the new heavenly Jerusalem (City of Peace) in God's eternal kingdom of divine love, truth, and freedom on an utterly transformed Earth—that is, completion, perfection, and fulfillment of the Divine Plan and Will of Divine Love in each of us as a fully evolved noospheric reality in Christ.

What this would or will be like we may scarce imagine. We may only say that it will be something wonderful beyond our ability to imagine in our present reality and stages of evolving consciousness. It shall be an inconceivable spiritual communion of love, bliss, and nondual oneness multiplied to infinity and perfection in the unity of the Limitless Light of eternal love permeating everything.

V

Tielhard de Chardin's Curve of Evolution—running from its South-Pole point of origins to its Equator, and up to its North Pole or Omega Point—gives us a relatively simple map of where created reality's energy has come thus far on Earth, and of where it's intended by the Will of Divine Love to evolve in the future. The outwardly moving arc of expansion has carried evolution from the Curve's beginning at its bottom point-of-origin through the three basic stages of pre-living matter, living matter, and living matter with both instinctive and self-reflective consciousness to the midpoint or Equator of the Curve. These phases of evolution have occurred automatically over millions of years through a process of trial-and-error and growing complexity in the makeup of created forms in the grand experiment of God's Great Adventure on our planet.

Now that we're well into the stage of living-matter-with-consciousness, the movement of created reality's evolving energy up the arc of contraction from de Chardin's Equator to evolution's climactic Omega Point at the end of the Curve will not happen automatically. The dynamic of human free will has come into play and the process of evolving consciousness turning within to awaken—with God's help—into its spiritual center, needs our willing consent and cooperation, our burning aspiration, and heartfelt desire to become who we are as spiritual beings created in God's holy image. We, as a species, are currently stuck somewhere on the separate-self Equator of de Chardin's Curve of Evolution. A spiritual awakening of human consciousness into Divine Consciousness is needed if we're to evolve forward to Omega Point.

What is it that's keeping us stuck and perilously placed on a path of collective confusion and possible self-destruction? In a word or few, it's the dead weight of the false-self system complex in its shadow aspect that is influencing us all, individually and collectively, consciously and unconsciously. Thomas Keating's revelation of the false-self system—which has come from a creative synthesis of divine inspiration, his personal experience of the Christian spiritual journey, inter-religious dialogue, and his studies of developmental psychology, sociology, anthropology, human history, and developments in modern science—is a discovery of great practical value and importance for all spiritual seekers, the times we're living in, and the crises currently facing humanity. This is true because the model of the false-self system gets to the bottom of what is motivating unhealthy human behavior on all levels; it reveals the hidden causes of the various self-inflicted wounds and problems facing and threatening individual and collective humanity in the twenty-first century.

Some obvious examples of these problems are: environmental degradation motivated by corporate greed, carelessness, and lies to the public; hatred; war; corruption in places of authority, trust, and power; prejudice; inter-religious rivalries; social, political, and economic injustice; unnecessary misery and suffering in human life and relationships; etc. These are some observable, unhappy symptoms of a massive psycho-spiritual disease in the Noosphere that's afflicting humanity on all levels. The false-self system and its emotional happiness programs running out-of-control is the cause of these symptoms.[6] This is a fundamental reality and pathology of the human condition in the world today as seen by Spiritual Psychology. In traditional religious language, it's the archetypal conflict between Good and Evil, life and death, creation and destruction in the drama and game of God's Great Adventure.

Our consciousness may not evolve to its full potential without overcoming the negative influences of the false-self system within us and our slavish addictions to its emotional happiness programs. To gain freedom from the false self and its inherent limitations, we need to: 1) take personal responsibility by becoming consciously aware of our false-self happiness programs, the afflictive emotions attached to them, and the negative results this bondage creates in our life; and 2) we need to actively consent to and cooperate with the divine action working in us, in our life and relationships to heal the wounds and transform the patterns of our false self. We each need education about our false self and a practical program to dismantle it.

As Thomas Keating has said, the false self's childish demands, happiness programs, and afflictive emotions tend to bully and push us around, to secretly run and ruin our life. Each step in the process of our outgrowing the false self contributes to the evolution of our Planetary Consciousness and Noosphere because each step in eliminating our individual false self lightens the drag of its collective and regressive dead weight on the group soul of humanity. Thus, we each have a vital role to play in the evolution of human consciousness and our planetary Noosphere. Everyone's spiritual journey is meaningful and of immense value for the evolution of humanity and the fulfillment of its highest purpose in the drama and game of God's Great Adventure.

So long as the false-self system and its unconscious roots are intact, energized, and functioning in the human soul, there is a resistant drag on our consciousness and freedom to live in harmony with the Will of Divine Love. This is true for us both individually and collectively. Additionally, the consensus reality of modern cultural conditioning—based largely on the egocentric values of the false-self system, such as pursuing inordinate material wealth, unlimited self-indulgent pleasures, fame, and power—serves to reinforce the grip and drag of the false self on us from without. Hence, inner purification and healing in the soul's unconscious depths and conscious attitudes are essential prerequisites, if we're to be free to live permanently in the consciousness of our individual and collective Higher Self.

If our Planetary Consciousness, or Noosphere, is to evolve to Omega Point, the individual and collective false selves of humanity need to be healed and integrated into the loving consciousness of our spiritually awakened individual and collective true Self (the soul's inner Beauty Sphere or Christ). Considering overall humanity's present state of affairs, this could obviously take a very long time to come about—perhaps, as de Chardin suggests, millions of years or less—unless, by God's loving grace, there is some shortcut to the spiritual liberation and awakening of humanity's group soul, which there may well be if a small minority of us become conscious conduits for the Will of Divine Love on planet Earth.[7] In any case, one of the best things we all may do is to work on our own spiritual development through a life of prayer (relating to God), meditation (doing the wisdom), service, and cooperation with the divine action to heal and transform the dead weight and inner drag of our conscious and unconscious false-self systems.

In concluding his article, "Christianity and Evolution: Suggestions for a New Theology," Tielhard de Chardin stresses the central importance of our evolving in love:

> In the act of 'super-charity' all possible forms of intellection and volition can be foreseen as indefinitely capable of sublimation, of synthesis and (if I may use the word) of being "amortized." Love, in consequence, is undoubtedly the single higher form toward which, as they are transformed, all the other forms of spiritual energy converge—as one might expect in a universe built on the plane of union and by the forces of union.

Then, writing further on the same page regarding the maturation of a planetary Noosphere, de Chardin says, "This great phenomenon is intrinsically dependent on the development of the universal-Christ in our souls" (*Christianity and Evolution*, p. 186). This clearly points to the vital and essential role played by each human individual's personal spiritual development—as a contribution to the evolution of the whole—and it's what truly fulfills the Will of Divine Love in each of us.

The divinely inspired positive impetus and purpose of creation's transforming energy in God's Great Adventure is to evolve the diverse energies of pre-living matter and living matter up into more and more centers of evolving consciousness. The aim of these centers of evolving consciousness (evolving souls) is to move, first individually and then collectively, through our learning and growth process on the Equator of de Chardin's Curve and then up toward and into the Curve's climatic Omega Point where all souls converge in God. This is to happen through the gradual refining of human consciousness into Divine Consciousness, until everything finally becomes freed, fulfilled, and perfected in the non-dual divine Light, Life, and Love of God filling, overflowing, and uniting us all in Christ, the heart of all souls. Centering Prayer has much to contribute to this process.

De Chardin's Omega Point of Divine Love correlates to the Crown Sphere of each soul's microcosmic Tree of Life. Humanity's collective planetary Omega Point is consciousness evolution's non-dual magnetic drawing force of radiant Christ-energy. This living, conscious apex of the Noosphere grows stronger with the spiritual awakening of each new soul it attracts and inspires.

4

GOOD VERSUS EVIL:
THE ARCHETYPAL CONFLICT

I

As human beings, we are all born divided between two opposing spiritual principles and two corresponding instinctual attractions. In his book, *Beyond the Pleasure Principle*, Sigmund Freud
identifies our two opposing instinctual attractions as "the life instinct"
or "Pleasure Principle" (*Eros*) and the "Death Instinct" (*Thanatos*).[1]
In the Bible and other sacred writings, the two opposing spiritual
principles in created reality and God's Great Adventure are traditionally knows as "Good versus Evil."[2] The duality of Good versus Evil
expresses an unavoidable archetypal conflict that's inherent to human
nature. There's a primal part of each soul that's attracted to Good
and there's an opposing part that's attracted to Evil. Our attractions
to these opposing spiritual principles and the conflicts they generate
create considerable drama—both comic and tragic—in human life
and God's Great Adventure. Good and Evil are often intertwined and
confused in creation's drama as principles of affirmation and negation, life and death, honesty and dishonesty, kindness and cruelty.

Being born divided between two opposing spiritual principles to
which we're inherently attracted is the basis of our individual free
will on the moral/ethical level. In the Bible and elsewhere, "Good"
(which is in harmony with God's Will) and "Evil" (which opposes
God's Will) are associated with the spiritual principles of light and
darkness, and their conflict is described as one of universal cosmic
proportions.[3] This dualistic interpretation of creation, religion, and
"Good versus Evil," which is relatively universal among Christians,

Jews, Muslims, and others, has grown out of reflections on human life and the warrior stage of evolving consciousness that emerged around 10,000 years ago.[4] "Good versus Evil" may be seen as the ultimate conflict in God's Great Adventure. Like all dualistic pairs of opposites, Good and Evil, light and darkness are relative to each other and mutually interdependent; for it's only in terms of their contrasting differences in relation to each other that they may be distinguished in the realm of appearances (created reality). This is the realm of our relative free will as players on the stage of God's Great Adventure.

In speaking of "Good versus Evil" as a dualistic pair of opposites, we are speaking of *relative good* and *relative evil*. Everything that's relative is variable and subject to change. This is one of the universal characteristics of everything existing in created reality. Created reality, God's Great Adventure, is a great dance of energy in motion manifesting the possibilities of what may happen, or appear to happen, in the drama and game of God's creation. "Energy in motion" means change and variability. Hence, everything manifesting in created reality is relative and subject to change; though the physical and spiritual Laws governing created reality are not so relative. These Laws are the expression of God's Will, the Will of Divine Love that allows for the expression of *all* possibilities within its creation: hence, Good versus Evil.

Divine Love is a great mystery that we know relatively little about. It is the mystery of God or non-created Reality. While everything in created reality is relative, God—the Mystery of Divine Love—is not. God is Absolute. One thing we do know about Divine Love is that it is the spiritual glue of non-duality that integrates and unites everything into an inconceivable oneness that has no opposite. All pairs of opposites exist within the realm of duality, which is the realm of created reality. Hence, all opposites are relative. Divine Love is ultimate or absolute Goodness and has no opposite. As the relative Good in created reality evolves, it evolves toward the absolute goodness of Divine Love. This is the positive movement of creation's energy in us as souls of evolving consciousness on our spiritual journey of return to our Source. It is the fulfillment of God's Divine Plan for the perfection of God's creation.

All of the energy and souls in created reality, which are far more than we may imagine, are programmed with an irresistible impetus of longing to return from the divided, incomplete state of created reality back into the loving oneness and fullness of non-created Reality. The path of evolution, which is the way of the principle of Good, is the positive way of doing this in accord with the Will of Divine Love. The path of Evil, which leads down into disintegration, death, and destruction, is the negative way of doing this. There are thus two opposite ways in which creation's energy may return from relative created reality back into non-created Reality, which is Absolute Reality.

Divine Love is absolute goodness, perfect, eternal, and non-created. There may be no absolute Evil because evil is a created thing and evil is the path of corruption, degradation, perversion, disintegration, and destruction. Evil says "No" to life, existence, consciousness, and God's Divine Plan. While Good says "Yes" to conscious existence and chooses "to be," Evil chooses "not to be." Hence, in approaching its absolute state, Evil self-destructs via the power of its own negativity, destroying others and itself (in that order) in order to return to non-created Reality.[5]

The two points of return from created reality back into non-created Reality are represented on the Qabalistic Tree of Life at the top and bottom of the Tree. Each soul's spiritual evolution from human ground in the Kingdom Sphere and Personality/Astral Triad up through spiritual ground in the Spiritual/Moral and Supernal Triads of the Tree culminates in the Crown Sphere at the top of the Tree. This Crown Sphere, which manifests the Cosmic Consciousness of non-dual oneness and Divine Love throughout created reality, connects into the Limitless Light of God or non-created Reality and is thus the positive point of return into the eternal perfection of Divine Consciousness. At the bottom of the Tree, beneath the Kingdom Sphere, is Evil's negative point of return into non-created Reality for creation's irredeemable and deranged energies. This negative point of return is an abyss of disintegrating darkness and unconsciousness (the complementary opposite of the positive point of return). It is the final destination of the self-negating path of Evil.

In traditional Qabalistic teaching, the negative point of return into non-created Reality has been called the "Qlippoth" or "shells of death." The Qlippoth equates to "Gehenna," "the hell of fire" and "place of destruction" Jesus mentions in Matthew 18:9 and 7:13–14. It is like a waste can or recycling bin for created reality's failed experiments, a psycho-spiritual black hole (corresponding to psychotic disintegration) wherein all that's divorced from the divine indwelling, filled with self-hatred and incapable of evolving back up the Tree is gradually broken down, stripped of its distinguishing characteristics and then disintegrated into unconsciousness for return through created reality's "dark gate" back into the eternal perfection of non-created Reality. This negative destiny is the natural consequence of choosing "not to be" and saying "No" to life, consciousness, and God's plan for creation's perfection that is the path of the Good.

The fundamental difference between the two ways of return into non-created Reality is that the negative path of Evil is by way of unconsciousness (like falling asleep and never knowing the difference) and the positive path of Good is by way of the evolution of consciousness into the immortal love, truth, and freedom of non-created Reality, which, transcending creation, may be neither increased nor decreased by whichever way an individual consciousness chooses to go. This is a paradox of divine non-duality. The Will of Divine Love gives us liberty to choose, yes or no, by inviting us into the divine relationship. We are free to accept or reject this invitation. As a consequence of being created by God in the divine image, we have the power and need to create on all levels of human ground (and perhaps beyond). We are responsible for all of our creations. My sense is that it is only our faulty creations apart from the divine image in us, and not God's creations, that end up returning to non-created Reality through total disintegration via the dark gate of the Qlippoth.

II

In manifesting created reality within the Divine Consciousness, the inconceivable Limitless Light of non-created Reality (God) has, of necessity, entered into limitation under the Principle of Duality and the pairs of opposites.[6] In allowing for the expression of *all* relative possibilities in created reality, God, the universal consciousness, has created the context for experiencing all the ways in which it is possible to not be God. This is happening through each individual soul on this Earth and throughout the infinite Universe of God's creation. Hence, the universal Divine Consciousness is one with its creation, intimate with everyone and everything, and living our lives with us in a secret, hidden way we normally cannot perceive. We are always in God's loving presence and God is always fully present to each of us, inviting us into deeper relationship. This is a fundamental, though rarely recognized, spiritual truth of our soul's life and existence: We are all in God and God is in all of us.

In order to discover all the ways it's possible to not be God, the Divine Consciousness has created or given rise to a great play or drama within its creation and in each individual soul created in the divine image. As consciousness evolves in individual beings, this drama arises out of the play of the pairs of opposites—beginning with the universal survival instinct in living organisms and evolving, as reflective self-consciousness appears, onto the stage of moral/ethical choices. Reflective self-consciousness with moral/ethical alternatives is the genesis of the archetypal conflict of Good versus Evil in which we all inevitably participate through our existential choices in the drama and game of God's Great Adventure.

We are all players in this game, each of us the center of our own individual drama and story. Each soul is equipped with all the elements and energies required for the universal drama and its tragic-comic possibilities to take place in us and our consciousness. The circumstances of our life situations and personal relationships create the outer, environmental stage where we may act in our drama and experience its unfolding. Our drama has meaning for us to the degree that we are actively involved, committed, and care about what happens in it. Drama is created by uncertainty, choices, and desire, by pleasure and pain, unexpected outcomes, and by contrasts of harmony, conflict, and struggle. Drama requires a story line or plot. Conflict—especially the Good-versus-Evil conflict in its many variations—always makes the plot more interesting, suspenseful, and dramatic. The opposite of drama in our life is abiding effortlessly in the transcendent peace, serenity, and freedom of our deep inner Self.

The principles of "Good and Evil" are quite simple and obvious as isolated polar opposites; but how they play out in our individual and collective dramas is not so simple because we are all relative combinations of both good and evil tendencies that war against each other within us; at least until we outgrow our inner spiritual conflict and, by God's grace and our good efforts, become fully aligned and in harmony with our true spiritual conscience and the Will of Divine Love within us. Outgrowing our inner spiritual conflict correlates to spiritual maturity and requires deep healing in the soul. This involves meeting our healthy instinctual needs and outgrowing the childish emotional happiness programs of our false-self system. The unhealthy motivational agendas of our false self grow out of our unhealed inner wounds, emotional immaturity and tendencies toward egocentric self-ishness.[7] It is these that keep us stuck and make us vulnerable to temptations to evil.

The conscious and unconscious desires of the wounded false self become top priorities that tend to run our life, often in spite of our conscious intentions to the contrary. As conscious or unconscious objects of ultimate emotional concern, the false self's happiness programs, in effect, function as substitutes for God, compelling us to pursue their satisfaction and fulfillment at all costs; even when this means going against our conscience. The false-self system—which distorts and exaggerates our basic instinctual needs for security/survival/safety, sensation/pleasure, affection/esteem/approval, power/control, and intimacy/belonging—is probably the most common source of the archetypal Good versus Evil conflict and drama in and among human individuals and groups. The false separate-self is, at root, a lie and its happiness programs are also lies that cannot deliver on what they promise, which is lasting happiness and fulfillment. At best, they may give us temporary happiness and fulfillment, if we get what we want from them. Ultimately, they frustrate and disappoint us.

Deception is obviously one of the means and ends employed and sought by the principle of Evil. One of Evil's common self-deceptions involves projecting our false self or shadow (our "evil") onto others.

This is a way of denying its presence in our self that allows us to feel "better" than others and perhaps justified in relating to others falsely because we may feel they are "the enemy" and deserve no better. This serves to dehumanize or demonize others (and ourselves), and prevents us from having compassion or identifying with others, which is a function of goodness in the soul. We are not meant to judge or project our negativity onto others who may seem antagonistic or different, but to love them as part of whom and what we are in Christ on the deepest, dearest level. Being truthful and loving toward others is the basic way of goodness, and this always fosters our spiritual growth—though it may, at times, cost us on the ego-level of worldly loss and gain.

We may unconsciously project our worst or our best, our evil or our good, our shadow or our sunshine onto select others we encounter in the drama and game of God's Great Adventure. The phenomenon of "falling in love" is a common dramatic example of this where the ideal of one's higher spiritual self is unconsciously projected onto another person, who becomes a captivating human god or goddess to us. This is equally as blinding, if not more so, as projecting our evil shadow so that, while the illusion lasts, the real person may not be perceived as he or she actually is.

In functioning under the compelling desires and mixed motivations of the false self, we tend to deceive both others and ourselves in hopes of getting what we want. Though we may or may not gain what we want in the game of our self-centered ego-drama, there's always a spiritual and mental-health price to pay whenever we compromise our integrity. Our psycho-spiritual wellbeing, health, growth, inner peace, and self-respect are always at stake—for better or worse—in the dramatic arena of moral/ethical choices that engage the archetypal conflict of Good versus Evil within and among us.

III

The dramatic conflict between Good and Evil in the human soul is well illustrated in a Native American story that's become popular among some prison inmates in Alaska, where I live. It concerns a tribal rite of passage from childhood into adulthood:

It was long the custom in a certain Indian tribe for the women to raise and care for both the male and female children until the boys entered the stage of puberty and were ready to begin their education and training for manhood, which they could receive only from the men of the tribe. Throughout childhood, these children were always surrounded by the people of their tribal village and had never experienced isolation or solitude. They had never been alone for any significant length of time and had always relied upon the stimulation and support of others around them who, as positive role models, nurtured and cared for them. This was known to be a good foundation for a young person's early development as a future loyal, honorable, and true adult member of the tribe.

Once a boy reached the age of around twelve years old, he had to leave the relatively carefree life of maternal care and childhood behind, and enter into his education and training for manhood under the supervision of the tribal elders and other men who were to be his teachers. He would learn the lore of the tribe, its history, myths, rituals, values, customs, and religious beliefs. He would develop the practical skills for survival, like tracking, hunting and fishing, self-defense, the construction and use of weapons, and all else required to be an adult member of his tribe. Once most of his education and training were complete, which required several years, the young man, now perhaps seventeen or eighteen years old, was required to go on and complete a Vision Quest, to finish his initiation and ritual right-of-passage into full tribal citizenship.

When he went on his Vision Quest, the young man would be spending a prolonged period alone in solitude, to test his skills of survival, reflect on his life, and go deeper into himself. He was required to go on foot and allowed to take only what he could carry and needed for his time in the wilderness—at least the period of two full moons or, if longer, until he received the vision that would guide him onto his life path as an adult member of the tribe. He had to remain in the same place, which could be a cave or a large hole in the ground, for the entire time of his Vision Quest.

He was required to keep a fire burning there at all times of day and night until his quest was complete. The only reasons he could leave his place of Vision Quest would be to collect more fuel for his fire, to obtain food and water from his immediate environment, or to go to the bathroom. Hopefully, there would be a source of fresh, clean water nearby. The young man was instructed to meditate on the flames and hot coals of his fire while he sat in his place of Vision Quest. This was similar to being in solitary confinement in a prison— except he was out in Nature, alone by choice and had the freedom to do what was needed in his own way.

Having lived his entire life up to this point in the company of other people who knew him, the young man was bound to go through an intense experience of social withdrawal that would force him to confront his existential aloneness/incompleteness in a very direct and dramatic manner. He would cry painful tears of loneliness and long deeply for contact with another human being, *any* human being. He would pass through a humiliating death of his ego that would teach him things which may not be learned in any other way about his needs and the value of human contact and friendship. He would wish beyond wanting for a friend to talk with, listen to, and share meaning in the moment. The poverty of loneliness in solitude can be a powerful teacher.

Like all effective ascetical practices, the privations of his vision-quest ordeal served to remove the normal outer distractions of daily life, forcing him to experience himself in a new, deeper way. By creating a psychic opening in his consciousness, the discipline of his Vision Quest would bring up into consciousness contents from deep inside him that lay hidden in sub-consciousness and the Unconscious. The young man's privations and practices included fasting; increased prayer, meditation, and introspection; and facing fears and aloneness.

In meditating on the flames of his fire, the young man would see the magic mirror of his mind reflected in dreamlike images of the soul's hidden depths. Hopes and fears of the past and present, memories of people, places, and experiences he's known, joy and sorrow, pleasure, pain, and images of desire would dance before him in the fleeting flames, disclosing him to himself. We never know what all's within us until we take a good deep look inside. The young man's Vision Quest was designed for this purpose as an ordeal of survival and self-testing.

As the days and nights continue on and on, and the layers of his soul are slowly peeled back in the flames, he awaits the coming of the light of his deep inner core that will bring him the vision of his future choices and soul mission, his higher purpose for life in this world as a man of his tribe. Who knows what he'll see or not see: warrior or healer, shaman or husband?

As the young man is about to leave on his Vision Quest, his mentor, the wise elder who has taught him the deeper truths of the tribe's ancient lore and religion, calls him aside for a final word of guidance to set him on his way. He says to the young man, "On your Vision Quest, in the flames of the fire you will meet two wolves: a good wolf and a bad wolf. These wolves live inside you as two parts of your soul that hate each other.

"Each of them wants to guide and control the path you shall walk in your life, the path of your choices. They are fighting with each other over you. The good wolf wants to guide you on the right path, the path of honesty, truth, love, and honor as a good and true man of our tribe. The way of the good wolf leads to more life, happiness, and the eternal blessings of the Great White Father who made us all. The bad wolf, on the other hand, wants to guide you into the path of Evil, the path of lies, greed, hatred, and violence. The bad wolf wants to trick you into following the wrong path, the path of slavery and death, of cruelty and destruction, sorrow and loneliness. These two wolves inside you are fighting to the death for control of your destiny. Take heed of them and choose wisely."

The young man is startled by this warning and asks his mentor, "Which wolf will win the fight they're having over me?"

The wise elder answers, "The one that you feed the most!"

We feed the two wolves through our choices and actions. The one that we feed the most is, of course, the one to which we give the most of our time and energy by following its lead, its inspirations and urging in selecting our choices in the drama of God's Great Adventure. Each wolf speaks and appeals to us through our feelings and desires, our emotions and imagination, our thoughts and attractions. As the inner attitude or spirit in which we act is the subjective focusing lens of attention and consciousness, the three interrelated Spheres of the Personality/Astral Triad on the Tree of Life within us are all involved in this dramatic process of conflict and choice between the good wolf and bad wolf in our soul.

For example, the energies, desires, and attractions of our animal soul in the instinctual Foundation Sphere of patterns supply the raw, unrefined passion and motivation that drive our behaviors from the automatic, subconscious level of spontaneous reactivity and conditioned responses; the thoughts and reasoning of our intellect and ego-identity in the Splendor Sphere supply the ideas and rationale for visioning, justifying, and pursuing our chosen desires; and the feelings, images, and will power of our emotional nature in the Victory Sphere supply the motivation and energy for choosing what we want and acting on our choices. Each wolf functions consciously and unconsciously in all three of these Spheres of the soul's personality.

Hence, the Personality/Astral Triad, in conjunction with the Kingdom Sphere of physical reality below it (our physical body, environment, and relationships), constitutes the dramatic battleground of the two wolves within and among us in the archetypal conflict of Good versus Evil. The Good/Evil conflict is limited to the four lower Spheres on the Tree of Life (Victory, Splendor, Foundation, and Kingdom). Evil—as a conscious or subconscious force in created reality—cannot enter into or function in the higher realms of spiritual light where the Will of Divine Love manifests openly on a conscious level. Evil may operate only in the secret shadows within the Personality/Astral Triad's Spheres while they remain clouded over and obscured by illusions of spiritual darkness, ignorance, and unconsciousness.

Evil may not function in the higher Spheres of the soul's Spiritual/Moral Triad where truth is revealed in the Light, Love, and Law of God under the rulership of Christ, the divine indwelling and Will of Divine Love in the soul's central Beauty Sphere. The disintegrating forces of darkness (Evil) cannot stand in the unifying presence and penetrating Love of Christ, which exposes all falsity and brings all truth to consciousness. In God's holy light, nothing may be hidden or concealed from the all-seeing eye of righteousness and justice in the Severity Sphere of wisdom awakened and innocence restored. As a rule, when Evil is exposed and recognized, its power decreases; when Goodness is discovered and recognized in the soul, its presence and power naturally increase.

Our spiritual journey is a continuing Vision Quest of lifelong pursuit. It is the path and gift of nonconceptual contemplation that brings our quest to its completion through the Holy Spirit's hidden presence and action deep within us. We may cross many deserts of privation and solitude, temptation and trial, failures and new beginnings as the good wolf and bad wolf battle it out inside us. Gradually, with patience, persistence, and God's grace working in us, we wear the bad wolf down—like an old pair of shoes—by depriving it of energy until it weakens out and dies or at least falls asleep like a dog in the sun. We may not know how far we've traveled on the journey of our Vision Quest—having seen few or no visions—but once the desert is crossed, the price of bad-wolf death paid, the soul laid bare and its inner heart opened; all of this changes and the soul's divine beloved appears as an invisible light of inner fullness crowned with treasures of tears in the love of our God. When the divine beloved so appears, the dry privations of stark solitude become the silent joys and breathless beauty of a new glorious solitude, peace, and goodness that remain alive in us forever, no matter what happens or where we go in our outer drama.

IV

Human ground is the dramatic battleground in our soul where Good versus Evil abides. On the Qabalistic Tree of Life, our human ground consists of the three Spheres of the Personality/Astral Triad (Foundation-Memory, Splendor-Intellect, Victory-Imagination), and the Kingdom Sphere of physical incarnation. Our perceptions and experiences of duality and creation's pairs of opposites are most pronounced in the Spheres of the Personality/Astral Triad and Kingdom Sphere. This is because the requirements of survival and the need to discriminate force us into duality in the Kingdom and Personality/Astral Spheres, where relationships arise and we need to distinguish one person or thing from another in order to function and interact effectively within our environment. Let us now take a brief look at the archetypal Good/Evil conflict in the interrelated Spheres of human ground as represented on the Tree of Life:

The principle of Good, which says "Yes" to life and others, affirms the beauty, value, and preciousness of creation in the Kingdom Sphere. It does this by noticing, appreciating, and caring for the various animate and inanimate objects of passing sensory experiences while discovering the presence of divine mystery in the wonders and Laws of Nature and the Universe, which may seem both impersonal and intimate. Conversely, the principle of Evil in the Kingdom Sphere takes a more utilitarian approach toward all objects of sensory experience (including other people), seeing nothing of value in them other than how they may be used to serve its own egocentric agendas. The principle of Evil in the physical Kingdom Sphere rejects spirituality as an illusion of wishful thinking and embraces atheistic philosophies of egoistic selfishness, competitive dualism, and scientific materialism as the only factual or practical ways of relating to created reality, which is regarded cynically as a random and ultimately meaningless accident of Nature.[8]

In the Foundation Sphere of the Personality/Astral Triad, the archetypal battle of Good versus Evil expresses as the spiritual struggle between freedom and slavery in the soul. It is the Foundation Sphere of memory that holds the programming of our instinctual nature (including our basic survival and reproductive instincts), our animal passions, our unconscious personality patterns, and all the habits of conscious thought, feeling, speech, and action that express our character as actors in life's drama. The patterns and habits in our Foundation Sphere function automatically and collectively determine whether we are evolving or devolving in our human and spiritual growth. Hence, this is a major, though largely unconscious, battleground between Good and Evil (or health and pathology) within us. The human soul's animal instincts, passions, and appetites in the Foundation Sphere need to be honored, domesticated, and brought into healthy expression, harmony, and alignment with our Higher Self, if Good is to prevail over Evil. Evil tends to reject, suppress, misuse, or pervert healthy expressions of life's basic instinctual drives in our personal life and drama.

In the Personality/Astral Triad's Splendor Sphere of intellect, the battle of Good versus Evil expresses as conflict between truth and lies, clear or confused thinking, and accurate, honest information versus false information. Splendor also involves the basic moral/ethical conflict between choosing to practice honesty or dishonesty in the pursuit of our desires and in our relations with self and others. We easily make mistakes when acting on false or insufficient information, even when we're endeavoring to be honest. An essential part of Evil's role in the drama and game of God's Great Adventure is to trick and deceive us with lies consisting of insufficient or misleading information. Whenever we deceive one another, we become, knowingly or unknowingly, agents of Evil.

Conscious choices are made in the Splendor Sphere of intellect based on the trusted information in our consciousness. If we don't have the right information, then we can't make the right choices—unless we're very lucky or guided by a higher power of intuition (Spiritual/Moral Triad). An essential part of Evil's game is to enlist the powers of our intellectual faculty to rationalize, justify, and even glorify false-self motivations and Evil's agenda. Knowing the full Truth, which includes the moral/ethical character of our options *and* their consequences, is the antidote to Evil's lies and deceptions. This includes unmasking Evil and exposing it for what it is. Our inner voice of conscience (Severity Sphere) gives us truth in self-knowledge and the superior power of foresight in our Splendor Sphere.

The false self's emotional programs for happiness—to the degree we buy into them—are a dramatic example of false information (lies) having a deceiving and devastating effect on our choices and lives in the service of Evil. Ignorance, superstitious beliefs, and all lies of false information are the allies of Evil in the Splendor Sphere of intellect. Self-knowledge, clear self-awareness, and the truth of accurate information are allies of the Good in our soul's Splendor Sphere. The self-centered "I am" of isolated absolute ego-identity that arises in the Sphere of intellect is the root-lie of all self-deceptions. It is a false, one-sided substitute and illusory reflection of the true "I am" of the Higher

Self or inner Christ abiding in the higher central Beauty Sphere of the soul's Spiritual/Moral Triad. Evil inspires and feeds on the negativities of cynicism, doubt, and lies in the Splendor Sphere. Good, on the other hand, awakens and grows in the positive climate of open-mindedness, receptive faith, enthusiasm, positive inspirations, and truth-trusting honesty in the soul's Sphere of intellect.

The Victory Sphere of human emotions, desires, imagination, and will is where Good versus Evil manifests as love versus hate in the drama and game of God's Great Adventure. The way of relative Goodness leads us gradually into the fullness of Divine Love; and the path of relative Evil leads us blindly into false love and hatred. This is because Evil, if we place our trust in its lies and deceptions, will inevitably betray, wound, and disappoint us. Here, of course, we're speaking of love and hate as a pair of relative dualistic opposites in created reality—as opposed to the non-dual Absolute Love and Goodness of God or non-created Reality (which has no equal or opposite).

The Victory Sphere is so called because it's associated with getting what we want or love. This is the case whether what we desire and how we pursue it are of Good or of Evil. Desire and morality collide and temptations arise whenever our desire to get something we want challenges our desire to do what's right and in harmony with Goodness; then we experience the archetypal conflict of Good versus Evil within and among us. When we have to sacrifice either what we desire or our integrity to get what we want, then the good wolf, the bad wolf, or maybe both of them in us are bound to suffer disappointment. In such cases, our decision-making faculty of free will in the soul's Victory Sphere is forced to choose among competing emotions, desires, and attitudes. There's always a price to pay because it's not possible to satisfy both the good wolf and the bad wolf at the same time in a dualistic drama. If we choose the path of Evil and fail to get what we want, then both sides suffer.

The wisest and best thing is obviously to choose what is right and good to satisfy the good wolf in us. In doing so, we always gain spiritually and the bad wolf is weakened by our refusal to feed it by doing its will. We always end up feeling better about our self when we choose Good over the Evil. Whenever the bad wolf is defeated or frustrated, it becomes sad, angry, and will try to bite us, to make us share in the misery of its negativity, pain, and hatred.

Whenever our selfish desires are frustrated and the bad wolf bites, we may suffer persecution, attack, and domination by various afflictive emotions: such as pride, grief, anger, jealousy, envy, lust, greed, apathy, fear, guilt, and hatred. Such afflictive emotions biting into the soul in its Victory Sphere, if they're strong enough to overrule our better judgment, may compel us to act them out on self and others; thus feeding the bad wolf and increasing the power of Evil to run and ruin our life. If, on the other hand, our better angels prevail, we may abide in inner peace and freedom from this domination in spite of the bad wolf's protests and in spite of not getting what we wanted. This weakens the power of the bad wolf in us. The enslaving grip of Evil in our soul is perpetuated and strengthened by the pain and weakness of our unhealed wounds supported by ignorance, unconsciousness, lies, and hatred. This bondage of the suffering soul under Evil's shadow is weakened and overcome by our willing consent and cooperation in the healing and forgiveness of our wounds (and the bad wolf), inspired and enabled by the presence and action of God's love and goodness in us.

Thus, in the dramatic conflict of Good versus Evil in the soul's Personality/Astral Triad and Kingdom Sphere, we have, until our victory of integration and wholeness is won, a continual contention of the good forces of love, truth, and freedom versus the evil counterforces of hatred, lies, and slavery. How to resolve it? Duality (Good versus Evil) longs for non-duality as division longs for oneness and time for eternity. The soul may be complete in itself only by integrating *all* of its divided energies and parts. Divine Love is the soul-force of intimacy, unity, and the spiritual glue of non-dual Oneness that integrates the soul in the liberating truth of its inconceivable Source.

V

Evil may not function in opposition to Good above the level of the Personality/Astral Triad. Spiritual ground (the Spiritual/Moral and Supernal Triads) is our soul's palace of freedom and victory. When

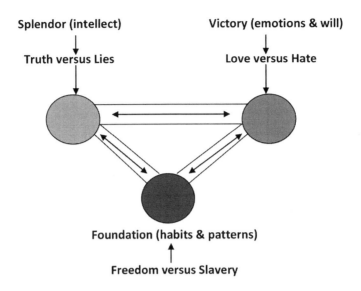

Good versus Evil in the Soul's Personality/Astral Triad

our human ground comes into full harmony and alignment with our spiritual ground, then the victory of Good over Evil is complete in us. That is, as our human ground is gradually integrated into our spiritual ground (and vice versa), the archetypal battle of Good versus Evil is finally won and the soul's inner enemy or adversary (bad wolf) is healed and transformed or else defeated and vanquished into the disintegrating abyss of the Qlippoth beneath the Tree in our soul. However, this does not happen overnight. It's a detailed and generally lengthy process. Only God knows when it's complete.

The archetypal battle of Good versus Evil in the human soul is as old as time in the history of humanity, which is punctuated with recurring cycles of war, suffering, and wasted life brought on by the ignorance and ill will of hatred, lies, and slavery (the means and ends of Evil). It's been said that "the course of time is marked by ruins, but beyond every ruin one sees reappear the dawn of hope or the twilight of deception"[9]—that is, a new promise of rising into the true light of spiritual freedom, or a deceptive falling into the old false darkness of spiritual slavery under new appearances of counterfeit goodness. These words identify the recurring pattern of the archetypal battle in our individual and collective souls, the two paths of the good wolf and the bad wolf that lead to positive self-creation or negative self-destruction.

The struggle is hard and grows increasingly subtle in the repeating cycles of Good versus Evil (where hope and deception reappear) in the historical movements of souls and civilizations into and through the six stages of evolving consciousness (tribal, warrior, traditional, modern, postmodern, and integral). As the banner of the Good, woven in living symbols of the soul's highest hopes, promises, and potential, is carried forward in humanity's struggle to manifest the Will of Divine Love in this world, Evil always appears in new guises of deception, corruption, perversion, and brutality to block the way forward and subvert our spiritual progress. In natural opposition to Evil, love, truth, and freedom for all are the means and ends of the Good. These spiritual principles are meant to be awakened and fulfilled within the being and consciousness of individual souls and societies living in harmony with the Will of Divine Love.

The archetypal struggle of Good versus Evil is the soul's trying struggle for freedom. Evil will always mislead and betray us. Motivated by hatred, manipulating with lies, and creating slavish bondage to negative self-destructive behavior patterns in the souls of its victims, Evil's job is to mislead and betray us in the drama and game of God's Great Adventure. Our job as evolving souls is to learn the truth of this game and how to play it to our spiritual advantage. We may not effectively do this while we're overly identified with our separate-self sense, the drama we're in, or the role we're playing. Too much ego-identity blinds and limits us to dualistic perspectives of self and other, loss and gain, and the prejudicial priorities of unhealthy cultural conditioning and self-centered agendas, or false-self happiness programs.

We are not limited to the roles we play or the outcomes we experience. The false separate-self tends to over-identify with the drama and game of God's Great Adventure, and to overreact to what happens in it. When we are thus over-identified with the dramas and games in our lives, we tend to take them too seriously, thinking that this is all there is to reality; and we lose the deeper perspective of the divine presence in us and in everyone else. We forget the awareness of our inner relationship to God that is always ongoing beyond the changing events of dramas and games in our lives.

When we take our dramas too seriously, it's difficult to see or accept others as they are because we tend to judge them primarily in terms or whether or not they may contribute to the success of our chosen agendas. We do not relate to others for who or what they are as spiritual beings of intrinsic worth; that is, as ends in themselves. Instead, we relate to others on the basis of whether or not we think they can help us get what we want; that is, as means to be used for *our* selfish ends. This serves the anti-cause of Evil by dehumanizing others into mere objects and alienating us from them; thus setting us up for loneliness, discouragement, and defeat in the archetypal conflict of Good versus Evil. It separates us from the spirit of love and the Good, giving undue advantage to the principle of Evil. The principle of Evil is grounded in duality and the false assumption of self as an absolute ego-identity in relation to others. It's natural for Evil to deny or negate our identity with others as members of one human family and Mystical Body of Christ.

Each soul's inner Goodness or "Godness" affirms that underneath the various outer roles we play and the differences we perceive among us, we are all actually one and the same in the light, life, and love of non-created Reality. We are all divine spiritual beings beneath the mystifying masks of our external appearances and cultural conditioning. Echoes of this inner spiritual truth of our underlying unity and sameness with *all* others (including the so-called evil ones) may be heard and felt in the curtain calls and applause of an enthusiastic audience following the transporting enactment of a comic, tragic, or dramatic stage play where—after laughing with the clowns, hating the evildoers, and identifying with the protagonists, and so on—we recognize that all the actors who so convincingly played their assigned roles are in fact, on a deeper level, one with the audience and one with one another. This exhilarating experience of recognition and temporary transcendence following a drama's climax creates a communion of souls that reveals something essential about how it actually is in the "real" dramas of our lives in human ground. Here, as in a dramatic stage play, we (individually and collectively) may be awake or asleep to the divine inner light of love that unites us all as we play our separate roles in the Great Adventure of God's Consciousness now playing in created reality. The vital point for us is to not become over-identified with our separate parts or to take them too seriously, lest we forget our abiding inner common core and true identity as spiritual beings.

VI

The victory of Good over Evil is the victory of Divine Love. It is the victory of life-affirming creation over creation-negating destruction. Divine Love is a great mystery that we, as evolving souls, are here to learn about and grow up into by giving and receiving love on human levels and beyond. We do this by playing and experiencing our roles in various dramas, relationships, and situations in the game of God's Great Adventure. In my book, *The One Who Loves Us*, there's a chapter called "Three Grades of Love: *Bronze, Silver and Gold*." These are the ascending grades of evolving love through which we gradually learn of Love and grow-up into its holy Mystery within and among us.

Beyond the three grades of evolving love is the Divine Love of God, which does not evolve because it already and always is pure and perfect as the immortal light, life, and love of non-created Reality. In following our precious metals analogy, we refer to God's pure and perfect love as "platinum love." All the authentic love we humans may experience in the three grades of evolving love is a partial radiation of God's divine platinum love manifesting into created reality. In contrast and opposition to divine platinum love and the three grades of evolving love, all of which are expressions of the principle of the Good, there's a fourth kind of love that is no love at all. In keeping with our metallic analogy, this false, anti-love may be called "iron love." Iron love is Evil's perverted imitation of love that opposes and seeks to negate all authentic love. As Evil turns against the Will of Divine Love, iron love is the love of cruelty, destruction, and love of Evil for its own sake. This deranged and degrading love, if we may call it "love," is purely in the service of anger, hatred, and Evil.

Within the grades of evolving love, there are various degrees of ascending love; or, in the case of inverted iron love, descending degrees of moral/ethical corruption, degradation, perversion, and slavish bondage to patterns of self-destruction and the will of Evil. The degrees and grades of evolving love are like progressive steps in the ascent of love's unfolding revelation in the soul's movement through duality into non-duality. This is love's movement through evolving human ground into spiritual ground, where the soul grows whole and complete, strong and free in loving union with its Source. The devolving descent of iron love, on the other hand, is the soul's harrowing fall into deepening degrees of darkness, duality, and the hell of Evil; that is, into psychotic disintegration and chaos under the will of self-hatred; the deceptions of vain ego-fantasies, lies, and delusions; and the bondage of slavery to self-destructive habits of thought, feeling, speech, and action.

The first grade of evolving love, bronze love, is the love of self-centered desire. It is "me-centered," selfish, very dualistic and may, under certain unfavorable circumstances, devolve into iron love. Bronze love is the limited love of a child for what it desires. Bronze love as one's ultimate love is something that's normal and necessary in the development of children but shallow, unhealthy, and childish in the attitudes of adults. Bronze love is the love of sensual attractions, limitless pleasure seeking, and self-centered ego-fantasies in the motivations and desires of an individual—as, for example, in our childish pursuits of the false self's emotional programs for happiness. Because it's so strongly "me-centered," bronze love gives top priority to the fulfillment of one's own wishes and desires. It values others primarily on the dualistic basis of whether or not they are seen as potentially useful for serving the cause of fulfilling one's self-centered aims. Hence, bronze love is highly conditional and purely in the service of one's own quest for happiness and fulfillment.

In the second grade of evolving love, silver love, the focus moves from "me-centeredness" into the "we-centeredness" of two or more individuals in a mutual two-way relationship or group-identity of some kind—as in our social, political, economic, religious, cultural, racial, or national groups. The "we-centeredness" of silver love takes the separate-self out of the exclusively "me-centered" aloneness of bronze love into dyadic or group-ego relationships of shared mutual interest, identity and, hopefully, caring. This is where we begin to appreciate the simple fact that others too have feelings and desires that are important to them, just as our own feelings and desires are important to us. Thus, in silver love, we gradually develop our capacity for empathy and compassion in relation to others. This is an important step forward in our spiritual growth into goodness, as it teaches us to value the rights and needs of others around us. Silver love is thus the love of mutuality and relationship that becomes a practical foundation for morality and ethics in human ground and society.

The rewards of silver love, which include shared identity with the beloved "other," far transcend those of isolated, "me-centered" bronze love. It's in the caring and mutuality of silver love that we begin to sense that we are part of something greater than our isolated separate-self ego closed in on itself. In the ascending degrees of silver love, our heart expands to new heights of inspiration, joy, devotion, discovery, trust, and caring vulnerability through shared experiences of loving and being loved by others or another. This helps us to meet our basic instinctual need for intimacy/belonging, which is both a human social need and a deep spiritual need of the soul in relation to God and to significant others in our life.[10] Hence, in silver love we may begin to relate to God as the "beloved Other."

Gold love, which is "thee-centered," transcends both the "me-centeredness" or bronze love and the "we-centeredness" of silver love. In gold love, which is the complete opposite of bronze love, our focus is entirely on the wellbeing, goodness, and happiness of the beloved, irrespective of our own separate-self interests and desires. This is a most radical love. Gold love is totally self-giving and "for the other," who is ultimately not seen as "other" but as one with the self of the lover. Hence, gold love is ego-transcending and selfless because it places the beloved above one's self in terms of priorities and importance. Gold love inspires us to self-sacrifice for the sake of the beloved. The selfless love of parents for their children is a common example of gold love, as is God's unconditional love for us as God's spiritual children and heirs to God's kingdom of Universal Love. In our spiritual life, the ascending degrees of gold love correspond to the evolving degrees of mystical union with God in the love of Christ.

As gold love evolves, it moves from being centered in particular individuals or objects that are special to us into more universal degrees of identity with and compassion for all living beings. Perhaps the greatest example of universal gold/platinum love known to us is the sacrificial death of Jesus on the Cross of Christ for the purification, healing, and transformation of human nature into our divine nature. The perfection of gold love, as demonstrated in the life, teaching, death, and resurrection of Jesus Christ, evolves beyond created reality into union with platinum love in non-created Reality. The awakening of such love in the soul is what we all long for and are ultimately destined to evolve into as God's spiritual children created in the divine image. This is our divine inheritance and its realization in each soul fulfills the Will of Divine Love and God's plan for creation's perfection in each of us. Divine Love, which transcends created reality, is the Source and fulfillment of all Goodness.

VII

In stark contrast and deadly opposition to our divine inheritance of immortal Goodness is the degrading path of iron love and descent into Evil. Evil has both spiritual and terrestrial roots in the human soul. Its spiritual roots stem from the previously mentioned inherent desire of all energy in created reality to return to the primal wholeness of non-created Reality. Both Good and Evil seek return to non-created Reality, but by opposite routes. Thus we have a path of Light and a path of Darkness, a path of positive evolution, and one of negative devolution. The spiritual impetus of all energy in created reality to return to non-created Reality is the inherent drive of all in duality to seek return to non-duality. This drive for non-dual transcendence is something essential and unifying that Good and Evil share in common. That is, they have a common ultimate goal, but warring ways regarding how to reach this goal. The driving impetus for return to the wholeness of non-created Reality, and the two contrary ways of getting there constitute the spiritual basis of the archetypal Good versus Evil conflict.

The terrestrial roots of Good versus Evil in the human soul correlate to Sigmund Freud's ideas of the Pleasure Principle and Death Instinct that come from the evolutionary history of life on Earth. In *Beyond the Pleasure Principle*, Freud suggests that we are programmed by Nature to die just as we are programmed to live. In other words, our survival instinct has its complementary opposite in the Death Instinct. Iron love, which perverts, degrades, and abuses human instincts and behavior, is one-sidedly in the service of the Death Instinct as a path to destruction aimed at negating all positive values of life, love, and evolving consciousness.

Our basic drives for life and death, and our instinctual tendencies toward kindness and cruelty have evolved up the chain of evolution's ascent as Earth's diverse organisms have struggled and learned to survive, propagate, and to die in their environments. Kindness—which implements the Life Instinct—has evolved from group identity and the nurturing, care, and protection of offspring. The motive for instinctual kindness expresses the Life Instinct of survival as a strong sense of identification with one's offspring, family, tribe, and so forth. The protection of one's own may require hiding or fleeing from predators or else aggressively defending against them with cruelty, violence and whatever means necessary. Kindness and love naturally serve to unite us, whereas cruelty and hate divide us.

Cruelty implements the Death Instinct and is a natural expression of anger and hatred. In the case of carnivorous predators, the instincts of life and death are blended in such a way that survival (life) requires aggressive hunting, chasing, attacking, and killing (death) the animal's prey to eat and live. Aggression, cruelty, and violence within a single species are also involved in battling for dominance in mating rituals and group hierarchies. In various dramatic games of survival, cruelty, and violence have become associated with conquest, security, and pleasure, as well as with fear, panic, and victimization, thus spawning sadomasochism and the famous *fight or flight* response. The love and care of offspring and the brutality of jungle survival are part of our evolutionary heritage as primal antecedents to our own human tendencies toward kindness/cruelty, cooperation/competition, and various good/evil attitudes and actions that we may instinctively or subconsciously associate with victory or defeat in the drama and game of God's Great Adventure. The drama of Good versus Evil emerges whenever our animal instincts and higher morality collide in the conduct of human affairs and relationships.

Iron love thus has its origins in the spiritual and terrestrial roots and aim of Evil as described above. In iron love, Evil turns against the Will of Divine Love, which has allowed Evil to exist in created reality as a necessary foil or counter-tendency in the drama and game of God's Great Adventure. In human relationships, iron love is a counterfeit substitute for authentic intimacy, caring, trust, and vulnerability. It is a pathological degradation of "me-centered" bronze love that's rooted in fear of authentic intimacy; wounds of unresolved anger and hatred in the soul caused by earlier-life rejection, trauma, abuse, or neglect; and, by way of compensation, iron love manifests the deranged psychopathology of criminal minds and delight in cruelty, deception, and betrayal, as in sadomasochistic perversions of destruction and the worship of Evil (false gods).

As cruelty divides the ego from its objects, iron love increases the separate-self sense of duality for both perpetrator and victim. Rape, torture, and murder are primary expressions of iron love, as are war, prejudice, and hatred of the "evil other." Delighting in cruelty, destruction, and the suffering of others (sadism); degrading, poisoning, and spoiling the environment for material gain or as an end in itself; and seeking the ruin of others and one's self (masochism), are all anti-evolutionary hallmarks of perverted iron love in the service of Evil.

The agendas of Evil may be conscious or unconscious in those acting them out because the process of human descent into Evil generally does not begin as a conscious choice, is entered into with some reluctance (supported by various rationalizations, justifications, and claims of necessity); and is generally masked by a cloud of self-deceptions related to false-self happiness programs. In such cases, one's evil actions are used as a means to the ends of getting what one wants, rather than Evil being pursued for its own sake as an end in itself. At some point, however, assuming one continues down this dark path so as to make a habit of it, doing what is evil or unethical becomes subconsciously associated with feelings of temporary happiness and getting what one wants; and one begins to enjoy the drama, thrill, and game of doing evil as an end in itself.

A critical line is crossed as the "power of the dark side" lures the individual in with deceitful delusions of its seductive mystique as a means of compensating for inner feelings of inadequacy, weakness, and loneliness. Entering into this abyss of hatred, lies and slavery, moral corruption and self-undoing are guaranteed as one becomes bound to Evil and its perverse ways. In truth, there's nothing glamorous or romantic about the false mystique of iron love and Evil, which, when seen as they actually exist, are revealed to be quite banal, pseudo-revolutionary, and essentially a self-defeating charade of vain ego-fantasy and self-delusion misleading Evil's duped followers into sadomasochism's repulsive hellhole of self-hatred, psychotic disintegration, and ego-annihilation (i.e., the Qlippoth).

VIII

Evil, in its true nature, is about as glamorous, glorious, and exciting as the inside of a toilet bowl—for the home domain and destiny of Evil is the place for creation's indigestible waste products, the ultimate in bad taste. Evil is not limited to a particular place or personality, like Satan, Mara, Maya, or Ahriman, but is a universal and necessary principle of created reality that may be represented or personified by any number of anthropomorphic images. The principle of Evil may be served by many misguided minions in physical reality and in the Spheres of the Personality/Astral Triad. Evil, as well as Good, may function in *all* fields of human endeavor, from politics to religion, from law enforcement to rebellion, from war to medicine, from education to entertainment, from business to pleasure, and from the most personal and intimate to the most impersonal and detached. The Good-versus-Evil conflict is going on everywhere as competing spirits and agendas vie for dominion in the souls of struggling humanity.

The evil demons and pagan gods of ancient lore, the perverse devils and dark spirits of vices and corruption loose in the world today, are not God's faulty creations; they are ours, born out of the individual and collective sickness, savagery, hatred, greed, corruption, ignorance, and evil that may manifest in the human soul. As a natural consequence of being created in the divine image and likeness (Gen. 1:26–27), all humans are endowed with the godly power, urge, and need to create in the physical Kingdom Sphere (see how we've transformed our environment!) and the non-physical Spheres of the Personality/Astral Triad where the battle between Good and Evil is waged. These lower four Spheres of the human soul and God's creation on the Tree of Life are the ongoing metaphorical "garden of Eden" that we, as the souls of Adam and heirs of Christ, have been assigned "to till and keep" (Gen. 2:15) so that God's creation may be evolved to perfection.

We may not fulfill this higher destiny and responsibility as co-creators with God until the archetypal battle between Good and Evil in our individual and collective souls is resolved and the fruits of this victory (not its spoils) are manifesting in our awareness and reality. Given our ability and freedom to create as we will (whether knowingly or unknowingly), we are responsible for *all* we create in word, wish, deed, memory, intellect, and imagination. As Evil's lies and ways thrive in atmospheres of ignorance and superstition, we need to know and understand the truth of ourselves and God's Laws of Cosmic Justice in created reality, if we're to be free to fulfill our higher destiny in harmony with the divine plan.

Our habitual thoughts, feelings, desires, and actions give birth to non-physical offspring (angels, demons, and gods) in the Spheres of the Personality/Astral Triad. These entities are sustained by our energy and may take on a life of their own within our individual and collective souls as separate centers of will and consciousness. It is these separate centers of will and consciousness, created and sustained by the energies we consciously or unconsciously give them, that become the good or evil spiritual influences inhabiting our individual and collective souls. They are our creations, not God's, and we are responsible for them. Our creations are endowed with the power and strength of the feelings and intentions we put into them. They do not possess the divine image or indwelling of God's presence within them and may not generate their own energy—as we may through our inner connection to the divine. They are dependent on energy from us for sustenance. Some of them (those that express the principle of Goodness and are capable of evolving) may grow into harmony with the Will of Divine Love and thus share in the soul's spiritual awakening of evolving consciousness.

Once our non-physical creations take on a life of their own within and among us, they may operate independently of our individual will; since they then possess a will and awareness of their own. Like the good wolf and the bad wolf in the Native American story, the more energy we feed them, the stronger they become. When our evil, unhealthy tendencies or habits become stronger than our will to resist them, then we become their unwitting servants, slaves, and victims. This is why it's often so difficult for individuals to change habitual patterns of thought, feeling, speech, and action that sabotage their lives and relationships, even when they want and try to do so. The unconscious drive of the bad wolf, with its stronger energy, overrules the conscious intentions and desire of the individual or group to do what's right. The conscious non-physical evil entities of our faulty creations and false gods in the Spheres of the Personality/Astral Triad are essentially parasitic energy vampires that require the food of our devotion and worship (our continuing to serve and place preciousness into them) in order to live and stay strong. They are not independent self-existing beings but our unwitting creations seeking to dupe, possess, and rule over us.

Our faulty creations will die out, like the ancient gods of the Greeks and Romans, only when we stop feeding them energy, and when the divine action replaces them with new patterns that express the higher will of the good wolf in us. Like the weeds growing amongst the wheat in Jesus' famous parable (Matt. 13:24-30), at the time of harvest (physical death), when the soul returns to its roots in spiritual ground (the Spiritual/Moral and Supernal Triads), its being and awareness will separate from its dross of errors and Evil creations in the Personality/Astral Triad, and the soul's faulty creations shall be broken down, consumed, and destroyed in the fiery furnace and recycling bin of the Qlippoth at the bottom of the Tree beneath the Kingdom Sphere.

The path of Evil and iron love, grounded in seething hatred, deceptive lies, addictive slavery, and the repulsive perversions of sadomasochism, leads the soul and its consciousness down into the psychotic, disintegrating abyss of the Qlippoth. Yet, just as Jesus is said to have descended into hell to redeem the suffering souls of the dead, so may many fallen souls trapped in the disintegrating darkness of the Qlippoth be preserved and redeemed by the saving grace of Divine Love if they will, upon "hitting bottom," acknowledge the truth of their errors, repent of evil ways, and return to the light of the love that's within them. Every fallen soul may reclaim the glory of its divine inheritance by returning in humility, faith, forgiveness, and love to the light of God's image and likeness abiding ever-present in its true integral center.

The Lord destroys not His own divine image—in *any* soul. It's only if and when the ego's individual will and consciousness fully reject and sever their connection to the soul's spiritual ground and the divine indwelling, so as to become split off from the true center and identified with the soul's illusory evil creations in the Personality/Astral Triad, that consciousness may be separated, broken down, and destroyed (made unconscious) in the Qlippoth's fiery abyss of disintegrating darkness. So long as we are a whole soul connected to spiritual ground and the divine image within us, such destruction (which is the deranged will of Evil) may not become the final fate of our being and awareness. The nightmarish idea of hell as eternal damnation and unending torture for the soul is a dualistic, sadomasochistic falsehood of evil iron-love's invention that is as perverse and fearful as it is incompatible with the non-dual Will of Divine Love, Goodness, or any sane understanding of God as Love. It is a childish human projection of hatred, revenge, and refusal to forgive.

IX

God-the-Father's silent, loving presence and Divine Consciousness are witness to everything and everyone happening in the immeasurably vast field of God's creation. The Will of Divine Love is the secret, sacred presence behind and within the scenes of everything going on in the drama and game of God's Great Adventure. In human consciousness, Good and Evil are value judgments. Subjectively, they correlate to our individual likes and dislikes, our preferences, desires, and choices; all of which are arbitrary and relative to different individuals with different priorities and in different stages of evolving consciousness. Objectively, on the other hand, Good and Evil correlate to the Will of Divine Love in terms of God's Divine Plan for the evolution of human souls and consciousness into Divine Consciousness and the eternal values of love, truth, and freedom flourishing in the soul.

Whatever gives the universal morality (Goodness) and blessings of love, truth, and freedom to the soul is of the Good; and whatever deprives the soul of its growth in love, truth, and freedom is Evil. Love, truth, and freedom are the meaning and ends of divine Goodness. Hatred, lies, and slavery, on the other hand, are the meaning and ends of Evil supported by ignorance, superstition, and over-identification with the false separate-self sense of absolute ego-identity. In modern psychological terms, mental health, positive wellbeing, and sanity equate to the Good, and degenerative psychopathology equates to Evil. Each soul's challenge is to find the way through the maze of intertwined Good and Evil in the drama and game of God's Great Adventure. Fortunately, divine help is available to all of us, if we'll simply ask for it, trust it, follow and cooperate with it by doing our part. When we exercise our weaknesses, we make them stronger, our self weaker, and vice versa.

Since the attractions of Goodness are obvious, we may well or ill ask: what is the appeal of Evil? How does Evil attract and seduce its victims? In addition to the childish, self-centered emotional happiness programs that feed evil poison to the needy, hungry egos of our wounded souls, Evil offers promises of pleasure, fun, laughter, and excitement to make life thrilling and rewarding. From mischief to mayhem, playing evil games and jokes of deception and destruction can be fun when this gives us someone or something to laugh at (as most children discover early on in life). There's a very thin line between harmless games and tricks of fun and laughter, on the one hand, and those jokes and deceptions that are motivated by malice and cause serious harm to others, one's self or another, on the other.

As William Blake wisely wrote in his *Proverbs of Hell*, "Folly is the cloak of knavery."[11] Healthy humor is a creative affirmation of life's beauty and goodness that serves to counter-balance the negativities and stresses in our lives. When perverted by Evil, however, humor becomes a pathological affirmation of destruction and death (as in sadomasochism).

We may not fully understand the psychology of humor, comedy, and laughter in human ground without understanding the psychology of Evil. Humor is often invoked by paradox, contradiction, surprise, and delight. This includes both good humor and evil humor. Evil is the ultimate contradiction in created reality. As relative Good and relative Evil contradict each other, they create a fertile ground for both comedy and tragedy in human life. The elements of Good and Evil are complementary and interdependent in creating comedy, tragedy, drama and suspense, irony and ambiguity in God's Great Adventure.

The freedom of laughter is freedom to laugh at ourselves. Evil tends either to take itself far too seriously, or to take nothing seriously, rejecting all true values of meaning and Goodness. The right balance of good and evil elements is needed for good health and good humor, lest we be reduced by one-sided rigidity and self-suppression into tediously repetitive, boring, one-dimensional human beings. We all need some fun, play, enjoyment, and creative innovation in our lives, including enjoyment of some unexpected and harmless incongruous juxtapositions of people, places, and things. Evil is our friend *if* we know how to use it, as opposed to being used and degraded by it.

When we take ourselves too seriously, we forget that we're only players in the drama and game of God's Great Adventure along with everyone else, and not the whole show—though we certainly are the star in our own unique version of this universal play. If we take nothing seriously, then Evil triumphs because life becomes hollow, empty, meaningless, and bereft of value for us. Human life's meaning comes from whom or what we take seriously enough to care about; and love, the deepest caring and greatest Good, is the highest value of meaning and preciousness that we may experience and become. We are, in truth, spiritual beings united to God in the inner holy ground of universal love and immortal laughter. It is God, Who's full of surprises, that has and *is* the greatest goodwill and sense of humor beyond all categories of Good and Evil!

5

CENTERING PRAYER
AND SPIRITUAL PSYCHOLOGY

I

Centering Prayer is a simple method of daily practice for deep-ening our relationship with God. It's a method for accessing the gift of silent contemplation beyond thoughts, words, images, and particular acts of the will. The gift of this prayer is not something we do but something the Holy Spirit does in us with our willing consent and cooperation. Centering Prayer does not replace other ways of praying (relating to God) but complements them, adding a new, deeper dimension to our prayer life. It involves a subtle move-ment from conversation with God to silent inner communion. An inner disposition of listening and receptivity, grounded in humility and faith in the Lord's abiding presence within, supports us in this prayer, which initiates an inner dynamic of purification, healing, and transformation in the soul.

Our job in Centering Prayer is simply to show up faithfully for our daily prayer time (which is typically twice a day for twenty min-utes or longer), and to consent to being transformed by the divine action working in us. The actual work of transformation is God's job. Much of the Holy Spirit's work in us goes on "in secret," in our soul's unconscious inner depths to which we do not normally have conscious access. Thus, much of what happens in Centering Prayer is hidden, or "in secret," from the one who is doing the praying. Conse-quently, Centering Prayer needs faith and trust in the divine action at work in our soul on an unconscious level; it requires letting-go of our expectations for the prayer and accepting whatever happens or does not happen as being God's Will for us in the present moment. Centering Prayer works by God's grace and not by our efforts; and it works on God's terms, not ours. Hence, it involves dying to our self—that is, our false self. It's a practical way of "taking up our Cross and following Jesus" (Matt. 10:38–39).

A key scriptural source of Centering Prayer is Matthew 6:6, where Jesus instructs us: "When you pray, go into your inner room, close the door and pray to your Father who sees in secret; and your Father who sees in secret will reward you." Allegorically, the "inner room" represents the spiritual level of our being—the private inner space of our soul's heart and center. "Close the door" tells us to disengage from both outer and inner distractions (like the incessant inner dialogue of our self-talk); "pray to your Father, who is in secret" refers to an attitude of inner silence and receptive listening (nonconceptual contemplative prayer) in the most humble, loving, and silent presence of the One Divine Consciousness (Father), which is witness to and intimate with everything. The "reward" from our "Father, who sees in secret" is the wondrous work of psycho-spiritual cleaning, healing, and new-creation renewal that the Lord does in our soul over time. Our job here is to accept and trust whatever occurs during this process.

Centering Prayer is a contemporary expression of what was known in earlier times as "resting in God" (the classical Christian definition of silent contemplation), "Prayer of the Heart," "the Prayer of Quiet," and "the Prayer of Simplicity." It is totally in the service of God's agenda for our spiritual growth and consciousness evolution; that we may consciously choose to become the unique person the Lord intends us to become as a spiritual being created in the divine image and likeness (Gen. 1:26–27). God is inviting all of us to deepening levels of intimacy and relationship. How this relationship develops depends on how we choose to respond or not respond to the divine invitation.

The method of Centering Prayer as taught by Thomas Keating and Contemplative Outreach consists of Four Basic Guidelines that have been described and nuanced in a number of excellent books and videos concerning the practice of Centering Prayer.[1] These Four Guidelines are:

1. Choose a sacred word as the symbol of your intention to consent to God's presence and action within;

2. sitting comfortably with eyes closed, settle briefly and silently introduce the sacred word as the symbol of your consent to God's presence and action within;

3. when engaged with your thoughts (thoughts include body sensations, feelings, images, and reflections), return ever so gently to the sacred word;

4. at the end of the prayer period, remain in silence with eyes closed for a couple of minutes.

Centering Prayer is a very "hands-on" practice—we learn about and grow in this prayer by actually doing it. The above four guidelines are steps to gently direct us into the practice, which we learn by doing it faithfully each day and through our subtle and occasionally not so subtle interactions with the divine presence and action within us. The real teacher or master of Centering Prayer is the Father, Son, and Holy Spirit within and among us. Since we are unique individuals, all created in the same invisible divine image, the divine action works with each of us differently—depending on our personal history, needs, and makeup.

We are each known through and through, from the innermost center of our soul to its outermost periphery in physical time, by the loving divine presence within us. God knows us far better than we know ourselves and secretly shares intimately in all that we are, do, and experience. Likewise, the divine presence invites each of us into deepening levels of intimacy and relationship, so that we may grow to know ourselves more completely and come to share more and more fully in God's nature and consciousness as the divine action opens up these treasures within us. The grace of deepening love reveals the truth of our soul and evolves over time into intimate mutual sharing with God in non-dual oneness. The method and consent of Centering Prayer form a practical way of initiating, facilitating, and deepening this process within us. How the deepening process of our relationship with God unfolds in us is what Spiritual Psychology is ultimately all about; at least from our side of the divine relationship.

II

There are innumerable theories of human nature and human psychology. In fact, whether we realize it or not, each of us has to be our own psychologist or student of human nature in order to have some practical degree of self-understanding and understanding of others. Each person's understanding of human nature reflects her or his interpretations of the world we live in and is necessary for each of us to function and survive in human life. We often tend to assume that others think and feel as we do, which is not necessarily accurate. A basic question of human psychology is: Why do people think, feel, and act as they do? What really motivates human behavior? All of the innumerable theories of human nature and psychology are efforts to implicitly or explicitly answer this simple question. It comes down to the basic existential issue of *what do we each need and want*? What do we truly care about? What matters to us? In the answers to these questions lies whatever real meaning and value we may find and experience in life. Love, as the highest value of preciousness, is the ultimate meaning of life; and, as psychologist Eric Fromm wrote, "Love is the only sane answer to the problem of human existence."[2] In terms of Spiritual Psychology from the divine side of the eternal relationship we all have with God, the basic question may be: What motivates God's behavior? Why does God think, act, and feel as God does? Since "God is love" (1 John 4:16), the simple answer to this most profound of questions seems to be *divine love*; God is motivated by love as manifested through the Will of Divine Love. Everything else follows from this and is contained within it.

The first and greatest spirituality is the divine spirituality of non-created Reality. This is the Macro-Spirituality of God that does not evolve because it is already whole, complete, and perfect in itself. We may think of it as the self-existing, pure consciousness, and Limitless Light of Divine Love, but this is only a humanly created idea of God existing within created reality as a humble pointer toward God's infinite and inconceivable Ultimate Reality. We shall come to truly know the Macro-Spirituality of God or Ultimate Reality only through full, complete, and conscious union with it at the peak of our spiritual journey, in the fullness of our soul's transformation from human consciousness into divine consciousness.

In contrast to the Macro-Spirituality of God (perfect love, truth, and freedom beyond creation) is the micro-spirituality of our evolving souls within created reality (see diagram on page 112). Micro-spirituality includes *all* the attitudes, feelings, and motivations that may influence our perceptions, consciousness, and behavior in the drama and game of God's Great Adventure. Human micro-spirituality is a continuum of all the attitudes or spirits—ranging from dark to light—in which we may act or be motivated to express our self in human life. Micro-spirituality consists of the full range of good and evil intentions and actions of which we are capable.[3]

The spectrum of micro-spirituality reveals the full range of habitual patterns and free-will choices available to us as humans on the moral/ethical and spiritual levels of our being. The process of our spiritual growth and consciousness evolution involves the movement of our habitual spiritual patterns of thought, feeling, speech, and action from the darker into the brighter side of our individual micro-spirituality spectrum. This movement of the spirit in which we habitually act into the brighter side of our micro-spiritual spectrum continues, by God's grace and our willing cooperation, until our individual will ultimately comes into full and complete alignment with the Will of Divine Love in us. This occurs at the far end of the light side of our micro-spiritual continuum where the spiritual root of true perspective on reality emerges from the deepest center of our soul grounded in the Will of Divine Love. God's divine Macro-Spirituality and its relationship to our evolving micro-spirituality is a basic concept of Spiritual Psychology as presented in this book.

Returning to human psychology, in most cases it seems reasonable to assume that we are all seeking some measure of happiness and fulfillment in life. The effectiveness with which we pursue this quest depends on the quality of our personal self-knowledge, and on whether or not we've discovered and accepted the fact that we are both human beings and spiritual beings in God with human needs and spiritual needs.[4] If we pursue only human needs and desires—the wants of our human personality or separate-self sense—then, unless we grow whole in love, we shall not find lasting happiness, peace, or fulfillment. There will always be a hole in our soul, the haunting sense of something essential missing. The false-self system cannot possibly fulfill the needs of our soul because it does not sincerely recognize or address our true needs as spiritual beings; that is, our needs for love, righteousness, and intimacy with the divine within and among us. This is a fundamental principle of Spiritual Psychology that is typically neglected, ignored, or denied by the various theories and schools of Secular Psychology, which concern themselves primarily with the problems, desires, and comfort of the surface personality or separate-self ego apart from the soul's transpersonal spiritual ground and innermost true center.

Thomas Keating has called psychology "the handmaid of spirituality." Our spiritual growth emerges from within and out of our human development, which is its foundation in human ground. Yet spiritual development may occur in spite of our human frailties, flaws, and limitations, if we sincerely devote ourselves to the spiritual journey, its ideals and values. The first big step in the spiritual journey concerns the conflict between Good and Evil in the soul (see Chapter 4), and choosing again and again to follow our true innate conscience and the Laws of Cosmic Justice (e.g., basic ethics and morality). Our ongoing moral/ethical character development is the firm or fragile foundation of all our subsequent spiritual growth. So long as we're human, we have to make choices between right and wrong, honesty and dishonesty, Good and Evil in the conduct of our lives and in our dealings with others who—though not really "other" in the deeper truth of our soul's inner spiritual ground—are definitely "other" in the dualistic drama and game of God's Great Adventure where we live and act as human beings. Our core challenge is to integrate the soul's human and spiritual dimensions.

In a very real sense, Secular Psychology is preliminary to and preparation for Spiritual Psychology. What has come to be known as "Transpersonal Psychology" forms a link between Secular and Spiritual Psychology, since Transpersonal Psychology acknowledges and takes seriously both our human and spiritual dimensions.[5] Traditional Secular Psychology, on the other hand, concerns the health and integrity of the surface personality or ego and its effective functioning in society (which requires conformity to the dictates of society); while Spiritual Psychology (which includes our relationships with others) concerns our relationship to God plus the wellbeing and consciousness evolution of our soul as a whole. Hence, Spiritual Psychology, which may be identified with Transpersonal Psychology, includes and goes much deeper than the focus of Secular Psychology.

Spiritual Psychology penetrates into the unconscious depths and dynamics of the soul in its relationships to the changing human condition and in its eternal relationship with God. Spiritual Psychology does not focus on worldly goals but on the aim of integrating our human ground into our spiritual ground. In Spiritual Psychology, the personality is meant to become an instrument for the expression of our deep inner self or spiritual nature in the service of the Will of Divine Love. Union with God's love within us holds the greatest fulfillment and is the deepest conscious or unconscious longing of every soul created in the divine image (Gen. 1:27). Centering Prayer has a key role to play in the process of bringing about the renewal and transition of our identity and consciousness from the values and goals of the false-self personality in human ground into those of our true Self, or life in Christ in spiritual ground.

III

The inner work of Centering Prayer is the work God does in our soul "in secret" (Matt. 6:6). Our responsibility in the divine relationship/ partnership is twofold: first, we need to remain faithful to our daily practice of Centering Prayer; secondly, it requires that, trusting in the mysterious divine action, we consistently consent to being transformed by God's grace working in us and in our life. This process inevitably takes us through all the details of our unique micro-spirituality spectrum: from the darker areas of our diseased motivations and tendencies toward Evil; into our gray areas of conflicting agendas and mixed motivations; and ultimately into the awakening of our divine qualities, true Self, tendencies toward Good and longing for God in the brightening-light section of our unique micro-spiritual spectrum.

God's work in our soul takes us back and forth in alternating cycles among our strengths and weaknesses, as well as our wounded in-between places, until purification and healing are finally complete in us. Only God knows when this is.

We need to submit to and cooperate with this transformation process, if it is to continue. This means trusting the divine action enough to allow our self to become humble, vulnerable, and exposed to the dark side of our personality. Hence, the necessity of dropping our ego-defense mechanisms and consenting evermore fully to the divine action working in our soul as we wait humbly and lovingly on the Lord's hidden movements within us. On the Qabalistic Tree of Life, this hidden inner process is symbolized by the descent of Christ/Beauty from the central Sphere of the Spiritual/Moral Triad down into the Foundation Sphere of our unconscious memories, motivations, and habit patterns below in human ground and the Personality/Astral Triad (see diagrams on pages 7 and 32). These hidden habit patterns include those of our false-self system; unconscious patterns of thoughts, feelings, images, and desires that comprise the secret inner workings and limiting factors of our human personality.

With our willing consent and cooperation in Centering Prayer and daily life, the divine action works on these habit patterns to change them, gradually bringing our will into harmonious alignment with the Will of Divine Love manifesting in our soul. This passage from darkness into light is not a one-time event but a long-term process. It's a process of many recurring cycles of movements back and forth along our individual micro-spirituality continuum. It continues repeating over time until all the dark energies in the soul have been eliminated and destroyed in the Qlippoth (Dark Sphere of the Abyss below), or converted and liberated into energies of divine light and love in the Spiritual/Moral Triad above.[6] Christ within us is the "true vine" of which we are each a budding branch of evolving consciousness and life.

Jesus reveals this vital principle of Spiritual Psychology and the divine relationship in John 15:1–4, when he says, *"I am the true vine, and my Father is the vinegrower. He removes every branch in me that bears no fruit. Every branch that bears fruit he prunes to make it bear more fruit. You have already been cleansed by the word that I have spoken to you. Abide in me as I abide in you. Just as the branch cannot bear fruit by itself unless it abides in the vine, neither can you unless you abide in me.*" And in John 15:9: "*As the Father has loved me, so I have loved you; abide in my love.*"

Abiding consciously in Christ is a key to our spiritual growth. Through daily Centering Prayer practice, we are implicitly asking to be joined more fully to the vine of Christ and thereby brought into harmony and union with the Will of Divine Love. Abiding in God's ineffable presence is not dependent on having more and more sensational lights-on spiritual experiences that come and go, versus not having them. Abiding, the gift of contemplative life, is a continual relaxed dwelling in the subtle peace of preciousness that is always here and now within and around us—effortless, humble, simple, and true. We may come more fully into this quiet gift of God's grace once the archetypal conflict between Good and Evil has been resolved in our soul; and we're thus free from inner strife and more easily able to relax in our self, consciously discovering and abiding in the peace and preciousness that's already here within us.

Centering Prayer gradually gathers together and harmonizes the disparate energies of our soul so that we may effortlessly abide in this divine state as the obstacles to its awakening are removed by the divine action working in us. This is our growth in the love of Christ. As an inner letting-go practice, Centering Prayer allows God to be God in us with respect to our free will. The genius of this prayer is its consent, which gives the divine action permission to do its work in us. Love, truth, and freedom are three primary spiritual values that reflect the nature of non-created Reality, the psychology of God (if we may speak of such a thing). Thus, the divine action always respects our individual free will and needs our consent to make us into a "new creation" as intended by God. In cooperating with God we become co-creators with God.

From God's side of the relationship, each of us is loved utterly and completely by the Divine Consciousness as God's spiritual child created in the divine image. Our souls have been created for this Great Adventure so that God may live it through us, all of us, and share the Divine Love with us as our spiritual inheritance. Here is the goal of our evolution. The fulfillment of this intention in each of us is the Will of Divine Love and ultimate resolution to the drama and game of God's Great Adventure. This is never forced upon us because love, given and received in any relationship, has enduring meaning only when it's freely chosen.

Growing love, held in any good container, overflows its confines and is effusive of its Self. Hence, love, by its very nature, is forgiving, self-giving, and meant to be given to all without limit—if we may but learn to receive it with humble, grateful, and pure loving hearts. This holy process is the eventual fulfillment of God's plan in us, and it's the ultimate aim of Spiritual Psychology—love returning to its Source by giving of itself, to itself, within itself through our evolving souls. This is the fulfillment of all righteousness to be prayed and played in the drama and game of God's Great Adventure. To complete this prospect, we must negotiate, with God's help, the passage of Good versus Evil in our souls and in the world around us. We are meant to be co-creators with God in the completion of God's creation and ourselves. Hence, we have a job to do and to this end we have the practice and process of Centering Prayer, which is entry to and cooperation with the divine work of God in our soul and the world.

IV

If we absolutize the idea that "God is love" (1 John 4:8) and thus motivated by Divine Love, then what are some implications of this foundational truth? Our ability to answer this most important question depends on our perspective—where we're coming from on the micro-spirituality continuum—and on the accuracy and extent of our understanding of the nature of love, and of Divine Love in particular. We may understand the nature of love only to the degree that we've actually experienced it firsthand in our life. Every experience of authentic love we're blessed with is an experience of God that teaches us something about this sacred mystery. Love is endless and may not be reduced to logic or machinations of the intellect, though reason may certainly aid us in understanding conceptually what love is. Love's revelation comes to us suddenly and unexpectedly through intuitive psychic openings as an instant discovery of great preciousness and rich meaning involving full-hearted caring and being deeply cared for beyond any preconceived expectations. Love is the most precious gift we may receive.

Love alive in the soul is a grand revelation of sacred nobility, enriching and fulfilling us as it inspires and delights. Every authentic experience of love is an experience of God in some degree—relative to our receptivity and ability to respond in kind. Hence, there are many grades and degrees of evolving love through which the soul grows and unfolds on its journey into the pure and perfect love of non-created Reality. We have identified the three grades of evolving love as *bronze*, *silver* and *gold*; and the perfect Divine Love of God that does not evolve as *platinum love* (see *The One Who Loves Us*, pp. 71–74).

Our understanding of the nature of love depends on what we've experienced of love and upon the degree of evolving love into which our soul has awakened. Love changes everything in an instant, giving rise to inner freedom, fulfillment, and the spiritual root of true perspective on reality. It evolves consciousness from duality into non-duality, radically re-creating and gently revolutionizing how we see everyone and everything. Divine Love within and among us is the basic teaching and practice of Christian Spirituality. It is challenging, revolutionary and ultimately overthrows the tyrannical establishment and domination of the separate-self ego and its false-self system. Love alive in the soul moves us toward a true vision of reality according to the Will of Divine Love. Our challenge, as free-will human beings divided between attractions to Good and Evil, is to sustain and live true to love's trusting vision of non-dual oneness without regressing back into separate-self attitudes of insecurity, possessiveness, and doubt that resurrect and reinforce the false-self system in us.

What are some implications of the Will of Divine Love being the basic manifesting motive force of created reality? Ultimately, this insight has to be very good news because it means that the Creator is benevolent and *everything* created is held consciously in the secret embrace of divine holy Love, which is Absolute Reality. Created reality is a relative (the changing manifestation of God's

Absolute Divine Consciousness happening within the Divine Consciousness), since there can be naught outside of or beyond the Divine Consciousness. Otherwise, it would not be truly absolute. Divine Love is the highest intelligence, infinite, all-knowing, and utterly sufficient unto itself.

In entering into the limitations of created reality, God has taken a bold risk—at least to whatever degree it's possible for God to take a risk. The risk consists of relinquishing absolute control of creation by giving us free will and introducing an element of uncertainty into the drama and game of God's Great Adventure. What happens in creation depends on our choices as the forces of Good and Evil vie for dominion, not only on Earth but throughout creation in the free-will Spheres of physical reality (Kingdom Sphere) and the Personality/Astral Triad (Victory, Splendor, and Foundation). Relative outcomes in individual souls and God's Great Adventure on any given planet are not predetermined but depend on the choices of individual souls. This is true on all worlds throughout the Universe. In entering the Great Adventure of created reality, God has given away something (absolute control over outcomes) in order to potentially receive something wonderful back (the perfection and union of evolving souls in Divine Love). It is in this way that God's creation may be perfected in individual souls and the collective like a great work of art flourishing to completion in the Master's hand.

Each evolving soul on an individual world is plugged into its planetary Noosphere (see Chapter 3); and each planetary Noosphere is plugged into all individual souls participating in its evolution or devolution. It's always a reciprocal relationship of evolving consciousnesses where each individual part (soul) affects the whole (Noosphere) and the whole in turn affects each part. The natural development of a Noosphere, according to Tielhard de Chardin,[7] is its evolution into a collective Divine Consciousness of group oneness in non-dual love on a planetary scale. Such a grand evolutionary event constitutes a climactic fulfillment of the Will of Divine Love—the Second Coming of Christ, in the perfection of God's creation on a particular planet. Thus, the evolution of our planet's Noosphere both contributes to and depends upon the ongoing spiritual growth of each one of us. Hence, the more genuine love there is in the world, the more our planetary Noosphere evolves and the better off we all are. Through our Centering Prayer practice and growth in love, we are contributing to the wellbeing of all humanity and to the evolution of our planetary Noosphere. Each one of us has something of immense value to contribute to the wellbeing of the whole through our spiritual growth.

Uncertainties in the drama and game of God's Great Adventure are contained within the immutable Laws of Divine Cosmic Justice, which function in all realms of duality in the service of the Will of Divine Love. This is another important implication of Divine Love being the basic motive force of created reality. Hence, in God's creation, there is liberty in conformity with Law, and this Law is founded upon the principle of universal Divine Love—Christ, the Word whence created reality is manifesting; Christ, the inner light and "only Son of God" abiding in the heart of all souls (John 1:1–18). By this wonder of God's grace, there is ultimately a way in which everything fits together and works under the Will of Divine Love—though we, in our limited interpretations and understandings of love, may not yet be able to fully grasp it. After all, God is far greater than we are. Yet, in our soul's eventual union with Divine Love in Christ, the mysteries of love and creation shall one day all be revealed to us.

The many and far-reaching implications of "God is love" include the obvious fact that the Will of Divine Love allows for *everything* that is going on in the drama and game of God's Great Adventure— including the expressions of cruelty and Evil that create so much suffering, misery, and injustice in the human condition. We, as limited human beings, view reality from our limited perspectives within the great drama and game. Thus, we are aware of only a portion of all that is going on in God's creation and beyond. In Arabic, *"Allah akbar"* means "God is great!" Just how great we may scarcely know or imagine, given our limited ideas and concepts of Deity, which we tend to absolutize. How we think of and thus relate to God is an important part of Spiritual Psychology from our side of the divine relationship. Fortunately, the Divine Consciousness adapts to all of our limited views.

Our limited ideas of God certainly fall far short of the true reality, which is a reality of Limitless Light, Boundless Love and Absolute Consciousness beyond name and form. Many of our humanly created ideas of God are actually unconscious projections from the light or dark sides of our evolving micro-spirituality spectrums, illusory mirror reflections creating God in our own flawed images and likenesses, some of which come from the spiritual root of false perspectives arising on the dark side of our micro-spirituality. One extreme example of this is the cruel and fearsome idea of "eternal damnation in the fires of hell" for sinners and non-believers who do not subscribe to a particular interpretation of God and God's Will. Such dualistic beliefs, which are really quite perverse and sadomasochistic, fall pathetically short of and contradict the non-dual magnanimity and greatness of God's Eternal Love. As God's spiritual children created in the divine image, on the deepest level we are all one in God and with God. Thus, whatever happens to us, in time or eternity, happens to God's golden-rule divine Self in us as well.

Humanly created ideas of eternal wrath limit God to created reality, underestimating the Divine Consciousness immeasurably, and, from a genuinely loving dualistic perspective, may seem like crude insults to the one true God Who *is* Love. It's actually a projection for us to imagine that God is totally "Other" and vulnerable to insults— as we would be. As non-dual oneness and Divine Love beyond and within creation, God cannot be vulnerable to insults because God is not a separate-self ego-entity with a human-like personality and temperament. Such phenomena fall within the realm of created reality. God's human instruments—prophets, saints, seers, enlightened souls, spiritual teachers, and religious leaders—may be vulnerable to various afflictive emotions, but God as non-created Reality is not.

Various flawed and limited human projections and ideas of God as angry, punishing, and wrathful were perhaps originally conceived in the anger, fear, superstition, and hatred of un-evolved tribal or warrior consciousness, as explanations for the needless cruelty, injustice, and sufferings created and experienced in human life. Trials and tribulations were considered to be God's Will and justice for those who displeased God. The Old Testament's "Book of Job," wherein

Job's friends were convinced Job had sinned against God, gives a clear example of this ancient belief. Such limiting ideas of God were subsequently hallowed by tradition, carried forward in time, and are still given prominence in today's tribal, warrior, and traditional stages of religious conditioning—where traditional dogmas and external authorities that teach them have the first and final say in matters of religious faith and practice. The contradiction between "God is love" and "eternal damnation" as an objective reality is somehow overlooked, ignored, or subjected to a rigid set of qualifying conditions (e.g., "God loves only baptized Christians who accept Jesus Christ as their personal savior").

We may see the evolutionary process of different ideas of Deity unfolding in the Bible by comparing the different ways in which God is conceived and presented throughout the Old Testament writings, and then in the New Testament by Jesus and his followers; there is a capricious, temperamental tribal God (who, for example, destroyed the world with a great flood in the time of Noah; and incinerated Sodom and Gomorrah in the time of Abraham); a wrathful warrior God of violence, conquest and destruction (who freed the Israelites from slavery in Egypt and led them to victory in a series of bloody battles that sometimes included slaughtering innocent women and children (e.g., Moses against the Midianites in Numbers 31:1–41, and Joshua at Jericho); a traditional-stage God of Law and Order (introduced by Moses with the ten Commandments); and finally the integral-stage God of Love and Forgiveness revealed by Jesus and interpreted by his followers (some of whom, using literal interpretations of Jesus' words as opposed to allegorical interpretations, regressed back into tribal and warrior stages with ideas of exclusivity and eternal damnation for non-believers). All of these disparate conceptions of Deity have been woven together in the Scriptures and carried forward in time as fundamental beliefs within the major traditions of Western Religion—Judaism, Christianity and Islam—often losing sight of or merely paying lip service to the greater unifying vision of God's mercy and all-inclusive Universal Love.

Certainly the God of Love and Forgiveness proclaimed by Jesus is far beyond the childish temper tantrums of a tribal god, or a warrior god's need for cruel revenge. It's not as if the loving God of non-created Reality is stuck in the victim-anger stage of the forgiveness process where one is obsessed with "getting even" to settle a score. Absolutizing such un-evolved ideas of God gives us a theology and a God that are sadly lesser than the true God of Divine Love.

As we read in James 5:11, "*The Lord is full of compassion and mercy.*" The group-mind thought-form of "eternal damnation," which comes from the false self and inspires so much fear-based religion—needs to be taken down and dismantled. We need to stop feeding it energy by worshipping and praying to it because it does not serve us well. It's an enemy, like "Frankenstein's Monster"[8] that humanity has inadvertently created since prehistoric times, and that belongs in the disintegrating abyss of the Qlippoth. Its ways and means are cruel, violent, rigidly judgmental (like a dictator or tyrant), and not the Will of Divine Love.

As Thomas Keating writes, fear tends to destroy relationships among people and nations. "It also destroys the relationship between us and God."[9] For this reason, it's important that we free ourselves from all theological errors and misunderstandings that inspire child-ish emotions of fear and terror in relation to God. Afflictive emotions of fear and terror breed mistrust, amplify our separate-self sense of ego, and tend to move us toward where we're most vulnerable to Evil on the irrational dark side of our personal micro-spirituality con-tinuum. As Thomas Keating points out, "*fear of the Lord*" in the Bible is a technical term that has nothing to do with the afflictive emotions of fear or dread in relation to God. Biblical "*fear of the Lord*" involves deeply felt attitudes of humility, awe, and reverence in relation to God; and giving top priority to having a right relationship with God, a relationship of faith, trust, intimacy, service, and love, as our Ultimate Concern in life. Our relationship with God is an eternal relationship of Divine Love that transcends created reality.

The horrors of hell—all the forms of misery, torment, pain, suffering, anguish, and tragedy that we may experience in feel-ing incomplete and separate from God—all take place within cre-ated reality. Since created reality is made up of energy in motion—and motion means change—everything in the great energy field of created reality (as represented, for example, by the Qabalistic Tree of Life), is ultimately impermanent and subject to the fruit of death/change. Hence, there can be no eternal hell in the literal, objective sense of a state of interminable suffering and misery that does not change and extends forever in time. Only the Divine Love and perfection of non-created Reality (God) is eternal in the literal, objective sense of the word. Reducing God to created reality equals reducing the Absolute to the relative.

However, hellish states may be *subjectively* experienced as eternal or absolute with "no way out in time or space."[10] It is in terms of subjective experiences that all possibilities of reality and experience are manifested in the relatively real drama and game of God's Great Adventure—where what seems to be absolutely real in the objective sense may actually be only relatively real in the subjective experience of an individual consciousness. This important insight points to the psychology of the complex dream of created reality happening in its innumerable individual versions (souls) within the One Divine Consciousness of non-created Reality. Each individual soul or stream of evolving consciousness is living out its own unique version of the Great Cosmic Dream as an individual player in the drama of God's Great Adventure; and we are all doing this together at the same time, sharing in a larger collective dream within the One Divine Consciousness. The Divine Consciousness is simultaneously living, knowing, and loving each of us completely in each moment of passing time.

V

The imperceptible presence of time within eternity, of created reality within non-created Reality, is a core implication of Divine Love being the basic motive force and governing principle of created reality. Divine Love is the ultimate meaning and fulfillment of created existence, and it's the task of religion to show people the way to this true meaning and fulfillment. All of the world's authentic religious and spiritual traditions are divinely inspired, humanly created, *kataphatic* filters of form through which the *apophatic* formless Mystery of non-created Reality may be worshipped and contacted as it expresses into created reality. All ideas and forms through which humans relate to God are symbolic pointers, seeds of the Mystery, and potential vehicles to help us access God's living reality. That is, they may help us access the non-created living presence of *apophatic* Divine Love and Consciousness that are eternally present within *and* beyond all manifestations of name, form, idea, and the energies of created reality.

A fundamental principle of conscious Spiritual Psychology is the core insight that the *kataphatic* forms through which we relate to God in word, image, thought or action are all within created reality and cannot possibly equal the *apophatic* non-created Reality that they serve and represent. They are visible clues of approach to the Mystery, but not the invisible Mystery Itself, which transcends name, concept, and form. It's into this living *apophatic* Reality that the method of Centering Prayer is designed to ultimately take us.

Centering Prayer is a journey into the *apophatic* dimension of relating to God, a journey of faith into the unknown Mystery of non-created Reality. *Apophatic* is a Greek word meaning "without images." *Kataphatic*, on the other hand, means "with images." These two Greek words represent the visible and the invisible. In terms of spiritual practices and worship, they translate into two complementary modes of meditation, prayer, or contemplation that may enrich, alternate, and complete each other when used separately at different times.

Kataphatic spiritual practices are active, concentrative, and employ the soul's faculties of imagination, intellect, and memory (e.g., the Victory, Splendor, and Foundation Spheres on the Tree of Life) as ways of relating to God. There are, thus, many *kataphatic* ways of praying, meditating, and contemplating, several of which engage our physical body and senses (Kingdom Sphere at the bottom of the Tree). These are the kinds of spiritual practices with which people are generally most familiar. They include but are not limited to: studying sacred texts, participating in religious services and rituals, going on pilgrimages, reciting verbal prayers and mantras, talking to God, musical worship, visualizing images and energy centers, breathing exercises, spiritual storytelling and dramas, creating or contemplating religious icons and art, works of kindness and service, examining our life and conscience in the light of spiritual values and aims. All such practices interact with the energies of the Unconscious and beneficially affect our soul's health and consciousness. *Kataphatic* forms of worship, prayer, and meditation are preparations for the deeper gift of *apophatic* contemplation.

Apophatic contemplation is a silent, receptive, relaxing movement into non-verbal, nonconceptual simplicity in the present moment. It's not something we do but a gift we receive. It's something God does in us, with our willing consent and cooperation. *Apophatic* prayer or contemplation is an opening to the mysterious movement of the Spirit in us; and Centering Prayer is a simple method of intent and consent that invites this movement by establishing space and conditions in us to render us open and available to receive this gift. In *apophatic* contemplation, the gift of God's presence and action works directly with the energies of the Unconscious and thus includes the divine psychotherapy as explained by Thomas Keating.[11] The Divine Therapy prepares us to increasingly receive and retain the gift of *apophatic* contemplation, which, as our subtle inner obstacles are removed, eventually becomes a way of life, the effortless way and gift of abiding in the peace and preciousness of God's presence and action in and around us.

With regular Centering Prayer practice, the gift of God's presence and action grows in us gradually over time. It grows as the Divine Therapy progresses and our inner resistances to the divine action are outgrown and overcome. A shift occurs in our inner motivations and attitudes, bringing us into the root of true perspective at the light end of our micro-spiritual spectrum. This inner transformation process is represented in various paradigms of spiritual growth and consciousness evolution.[12] Its completion is the critical *sine qua non* of our spiritual journey from false self into true Self, from ego to Enlightenment, from hatred, lies, and slavery into love, truth, and freedom. The way of our spiritual growth into full union with Christ is a progressive refinement of our individual will on both conscious and unconscious levels into deepening harmony and union with the Will of Divine Love.

The spiritual journey of our will and consciousness in Centering Prayer may be described in terms of a movement, initiated by the divine action, into and through three metaphorical Walls of prayer or meditation. These three Walls are: the Wall of Thoughts, the Wall of Energy, and the Wall of Silence.[13] As mentioned earlier, in Centering Prayer "thoughts" is an umbrella term that includes all categories of particular perceptions that we may experience—all that we see, hear smell, touch, taste, think, feel, say, do, and imagine within and around us. The Wall of Thoughts thus holds all the subjective and objective contents in our entire field of conscious awareness, plus the contents of our subconscious and the processes, images, and energies of the Unconscious. The Wall of Thoughts is vast and endless.

Underneath the Wall of Thoughts is the subtler Wall of Energy, out of which the Wall of Thoughts emerges. The Wall of Energy underlies phenomenal reality and has many gradations that unfold as the drama and game of God's Great Adventure evolves forward in time. The Wall of Energy remains unconscious much of the time but occasionally some of its contents become objects of our conscious perception. Whenever this happens, the Wall of Energy becomes part of the Wall of Thoughts. The Wall of Energy includes all the imaginable Spheres of emanation and activity of the Divine Consciousness on the Tree of Life, which is replicated in each evolving soul. The holy Spheres on the Tree (known as *chakras* in Eastern Traditions) are the subtle energy centers that constitute the soul's vital mechanisms and give rise to the various phenomena of consciousness and experience that we encounter within and around us in the Wall of Thoughts.

In most people, the Wall of Thoughts dominates consciousness and the Wall of Energy remains unconscious most of the time. Occasionally, the Wall of Energy is experienced spontaneously on a conscious level as vibrations, movements, and currents of energy in the physical body, consciousness, and nervous system (e.g., when we experience sexual arousal or strong emotions). There are also certain *kataphatic* meditation practices that bring the Wall of Energy into consciousness in the human soul through the use of visualizations, mantras, physical gestures, and the breath.[14] Such practices are specific techniques for awakening and directing the flow of specific subtle energies in the soul. These energies range from our instinctual animal passions in the Foundation Sphere (which need to be harmonized, tamed and refined)

to the higher refinements of righteousness and love in the Spiritual/
Moral Triad and beyond. All of this energy in motion evolving in the
soul is part of Spiritual Psychology.

In Centering Prayer, which is, of course, a receptive spiritual practice, we do not deliberately try to awaken the Wall of Energy. The aim
of Centering Prayer is to transcend the Walls of Thoughts and Energy
by disregarding them and relaxing into the Wall of Silence, which is
the quiet space between our thoughts, sensations, and perceptions.
Actually, this is not something we can bring about on our own. It's
something that only the divine action may bring about in us, as God
wills. Our job in Centering Prayer is simply to allow it to happen
whenever it does by consenting to and letting-go of *whatever* is happening in our field of conscious awareness. The rest (pun intended) is
up to God, not us.

There are times during Centering Prayer practice when some people may have spontaneous experiences of the Wall of Energy. This
may be part of the unloading process wherein energies stored in the
physical body and the Unconscious are released into consciousness.
Conscious experiences of the Wall of Energy bring us to the important distinction between "lights-on mysticism" and "lights-off mysticism."[15] Lights-on mysticism occurs whenever we have felt experiences of God's presence or action arising out of the Wall of Energy.
Such experiences may also include direct experiences of the psycho-
spiritual energy itself in its many variations. These would include feelings of deep peace, consolation, inspiration, love, visions, and various altered states of consciousness. If or when these experiences do
come to us in Centering Prayer, and they can be quite pleasurable and
attractive, we simply accept them as God's will for us in the present
moment, allowing them to come and go without clinging to them.
This letting-go of what is pleasurable is part of the discipline of Centering Prayer.

For most people practicing Centering Prayer, the spiritual journey
is a "lights-off" experience most of the time. That is, the Wall of
Energy remains mostly unconscious and there are not a lot of flashy
boats that come down the stream of consciousness in the forms of
lights-on mystical experiences, emotional consolations, and intuitive

revelations. This is actually a much safer path for those with the faith and devotion to persevere through apparent spiritual deserts, unloading of the Unconscious, and the absence of felt experiences of God's immediate presence. Lights-on experiences of the Wall of Energy may come from both the light and dark sides of the soul's micro-spirituality spectrum. That is, these extraordinary experiences may include inspirations of the Holy Spirit (God breathing new life into the soul), and a variety of intimate communications that originate in the soul's Spiritual/Moral Triad. On the other hand, some lights-on experiences are deceptive illusions and temptations that originate in the false-self shadows of the Personality/Astral Triad on the dark side of the micro-spiritual continuum. Hence, the vital need of detachment, inner purification, and healing of our inner wounds and unconscious motivations by the divine action working in us.

Lights-on experiences can be distracting for the false-self ego and may lead to delusions of self-importance and grandeur. An individual having lights-on experiences, whether coming from the dark or the light side of the micro-spirituality continuum, needs to both allow and detach from them before he or she may relax and gently enter into deeper prayer. Relaxing into the present moment in simplicity and silence in an attitude of humble consent is what *all* practitioners of Centering Prayer need to do. The safer path of lights-off mysticism certainly helps to keep one humble and offers a simple portal of entry into the Wall of Silence.

The Wall of Silence is the mysterious place of deep resting in God in effortless *apophatic* contemplation; that is, beyond, beneath, and within the Walls of Thoughts and Energy in receptive, nonconceptual prayer. It's always the divine action that brings us into this quiet, peaceful place of consciousness without an object. In the Wall of Silence, we know we're somewhere; that is, we're not unconscious; but we don't know where we are because there's no point of separate-self reference to distinguish one thing from another, and there are no things present! It's a place of sacred nothingness, meaning *no-thing-ness*, with little, if any, sense of time passing or anything else existing. The Walls of Energy and Thoughts are unconscious to us when we're immersed into the Wall of Silence. The moving Walls of Energy and

Thoughts are born out of the still Wall of Silence, which, though dark as a womb of creation, is paradoxically one with the luminous Limitless Light of non-created Reality.

The Wall of Silence is a place of passage and transition in the soul. Only the divine action can bring us there into this deep rest. The Wall of Silence corresponds to the dark, invisible Sphere on the Tree of Life, which I've called "Daath/the Cloud,"[16] after *The Cloud of Unknowing*, the anonymous fourteenth-century spiritual classic that's a primary source of the Centering Prayer method. The darkness of Daath/the Cloud is nothing like the dark side of the soul's micro-spirituality spectrum. There are different kinds of darkness. The darkness of Daath/the Cloud is a non-dual darkness that transcends the drama and game of God's Great Adventure and has no opposite; unlike the corrupt darkness of Evil that opposes Goodness and the righteous Light of Love, Truth, and Freedom.

The soul's entry into the Wall of Silence and its passage through the dark, invisible Sphere of Daath/the Cloud is traditionally associated with "crossing the Abyss" separating individual consciousness from the Universal Consciousness of the higher Spheres on the Tree of Life (see Chapter Eight). The soul's journey through the dark Sphere is generally long in terms of time and short in terms of distance—since everything is always already present here and now. The dark Sphere in the Wall of Silence is the "inner room" of the Divine Therapy where the crucial passage of the soul's inner transformation takes place.

This is a perilous passage of death and rebirth for the individual consciousness and the patterns of its personality construction. It correlates to the passive purifications of the dark nights described by John of the Cross[17] in which the soul submits to the inner work of the divine action. This is the work of spiritual healing and transformation done by the divine action in the soul's Unconscious via the consent of Centering Prayer and the deep rest of *apophatic* contemplation to which Centering Prayer gives access. It is the Divine Therapy of true Spiritual Psychology in action where we may not go up into the light of our soul's spiritual heights without first going down into the depths of its hidden unhealed darkness; before the inner resurrection comes the descent into hell. This is clearly represented in Thomas Keating's model of "the spiral staircase" in *Intimacy with God* (pp. 37–63).

VI

The drama and game of God's Great Adventure is wide open to *all* possibilities spanning the spectrum of the human soul's micro-spirituality. As this grand play of the Divine Consciousness embraces the full range of dramatic possibilities and our micro-spirituality, we each share in some portion of this great dance in the challenges and experiences of our lives, the pains and pleasures, inspirations and delights, the trials and heartbreaks we know as human beings. Creation's magnitude is too immense for mortal minds to fully grasp as we each experience God's Great Adventure from within our own limited, unique perspectives, which are conditioned by culture and the opposing roots of true and false perspective active in our souls. Only the Universal Consciousness and Macro-Spirituality of Divine Love may know the whole show as it happens and is happening.

Often we're caught up into and held captive by this Great Adventure in which we each play our personal parts as individual centers of consciousness. What our hearts desire and how we pursue this are core issues in each person's Spiritual Psychology: Is what we want truly good for us? Do we honor and respect the legitimate needs and rights of others in how we pursue our desires? These questions are answered by where the inspiration for our desires and actions comes from on our micro-spiritual continuum. Is it the bright root of true perspective at one end of the spectrum, the dark root of false perspective at the other extreme, or some combination of the two in the gray area between these extremes?

As thoughts circulate in the mind, moods change and different objects enter our field of awareness in the Wall of Thoughts, our heart moves about to different areas of the micro-spirituality spectrum, gravitating toward the light or dark ends of the spectrum. Most people are most of the time in the gray area between the extremes, feeling the pull of mixed inspirations of desire. As we evolve spiritually, our habitual center of attitude and consciousness gradually migrates closer to the root of true perspective at the light end of our micro-spiritual continuum. Conversely, when individual souls degenerate and gravitate toward Evil and absolutizing the separate-self sense, their spiritual center moves toward the skewed dark end of the spectrum— the root of false perspective.

Thus, there are innumerable perspectives through which we may view and respond to our self, our life, and the world. The root of false perspective lies at the extreme dark end of our micro-spiritual continuum. This is the dark root of ego-contraction that causes us to see the world through a lens of separate-self desires and emotional happiness programs. This orientation creates a narrowing down of our viewpoint into perspectives that look to egocentric desires as top priorities and sources of meaning, value, and fulfillment in life. Here, the tendency is to absolutize the importance of some particular self-centered desire or perspective to the exclusion of others. This colors our world with a blindfold of one-sided prejudice.

The root of true perspective springs from spiritual ground and resides on the extreme light end of our micro-spiritual continuum. This most righteous root causes us to view the world through the larger lens of the Will of Divine Love. In this view, the ego and its desires are greatly relativized and the needs and rights of all are prioritized on the basis of love for all. The root of true perspective opens our eyes and consciousness to a radically new way of seeing and being. In its purity and perfection, the root of true perspective is God's point of view; that is, the perspective of non-dual Universal Love for God's creation and all souls in it. As our soul evolves toward the light extreme of its micro-spiritual continuum, we may sense the root of true perspective rising from the Wall of Silence in the true center of our being. Our natural attitudes in daily life gradually change from ego-centeredness into those of the gospel values taught by Jesus and the fruits of the Spirit mentioned by Paul (Gal. 5:22–23). This is a gift of our deepening passage in Centering Prayer through the dark Sphere of Daath/the Cloud.

Daath/the Cloud of Unknowing in the Wall of Silence brings us to the point of transcending the drama and game of God's Great

Adventure through the gift of *apophatic* contemplation. This transcendence is a place of profound serenity and inner freedom in the root of true perspective where we find that all we need to feel whole and complete is already present within us—in our abiding relationship with the divine presence alive in our soul. Our experience of this blessed serene state—a gift of the divine in us—first appears intermittently, as the Divine Therapy continues in the Unconscious and we move closer to the root of true perspective. Gradually, our inner serenity grows stronger and manifests more frequently as we learn to let go of undue attachment to life's drama by abiding more and more in the peace and preciousness of the present moment—humble, simple, and true to the taste of what is. In this way, inner abiding and outer activity gradually evolve into a healthy unity of movement and rest in our life. Centering Prayer helps us to cultivate this precious gift—through the removal of its obstacles and the manifestation of its fruits in us.

The spiritual poise of inner peace given by God provides a counterbalance to the hurried business, stress, and distractions of being caught up in, over-identified with, and attached to our roles as actors in life's drama and game. To play our parts in God's Great Adventure most effectively, we need to draw inspiration and guidance from the root of true perspective within us. When we learn to rest in the root of true perspective, the Spirit is there to guide us in each detail of daily life, as well as into the depths of silent *apophatic* prayer in the Wall of Silence where we sink into communion and union with the divine within. It's a basic fact of human life that we are each responsible for our choices and bound to inherit the positive and negative fruits of our performances in the drama of God's Great Adventure—according to the Laws of Cosmic Justice under the Will of Divine Love.

VII

The root of true perspective gives rise to a state of consciousness that inspires righteous action in harmony with the Laws of Cosmic Justice. As Love determines Justice, so is honesty the road to Freedom. We need to be willing to face the full truth of our soul so that we may, with God's help, reclaim the parts of our self that are lost and trapped in the gray and dark areas of our micro-spiritual continuum. This process is aptly symbolized by Jesus' descent into hell after his death on the Cross and before his resurrection into eternal life on the new morning of Easter. The truth of our soul includes the hidden shames of its wounding that destroyed our primal innocence and purity of heart. Our soul's lost innocence and purity are redeemed and restored as we become whole in the Love of Christ.

The soul's allegorical descent into hell correlates to the unloading of the Unconscious in the Divine Therapy of Centering Prayer and is called "regression in the service of the ego" by Sigmund Freud in the Secular Psychology of Psychoanalysis. This regression or going back into previous stages of development expresses the need to redeem our personal history by revisiting the places where we were wounded and got stuck in our emotional, psychological, and spiritual development. The deep and thorough healing of these inner wounds is a primary aim of unloading the Unconscious in the Divine Therapy. It brings us to integral wholeness and prepares us for union with Christ. All that happens or doesn't happen in Centering Prayer is part of our journey into the Mystery of God.

As our inner obstacles to God are removed by the divine action, the root of true perspective grows humbly within us, enabling the soul to gradually receive the luminous vision of the Will of Divine Love. The new perspective of love changes everything. Love's spontaneous insight of realization awakens the soul to the preciousness of everything and everyone in God right now. The self-centered ego's normal viewpoint is astonished and transcended.

From the root of true perspective cultivated by the Divine Therapy springs the fountain of forgiveness that cleanses the soul of all bitterness and guilt. We see life with new eyes in the light of Divine Love, the holy preciousness of God's truth pervading created reality and giving ever-new life to the soul. This is the voice of our God, whispering silence through heart and mind to open the palace of peace in our soul's inner temple (1 Cor. 3:16), where awe, reverence and gratitude overflow with tears of blessing in love, joy, and the rewarding glad bliss of humble worship.

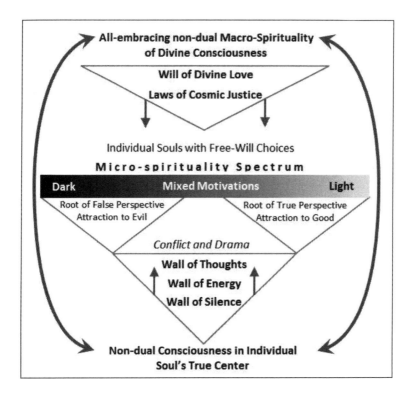

SPIRITUAL PSYCHOLOGY IN GOD'S GREAT ADVENTURE

The Wall of Thoughts (all particular perceptions) arises out of the underlying Wall of Energy that emerges from the Wall of Silence. The centering process of contemplative prayer reverses this movement, allowing us to eventually access the soul's true center through the door of interior silence and rest, which connects us back into the Macro-Spirituality of the Divine Consciousness wherein we dwell.

6

THE TRANSCENDENT FUNCTION

CENTERING PRAYER AND JUNGIAN PSYCHOLOGY

I

"The Transcendent Function" is a term coined in 1916 by Carl Gustav Jung (1875–1961), the great Swiss pioneer in depth psychology. Through his practice of Psychoanalysis (which he first learned from Sigmund Freud),[1] his work with analytical patients, and experimental researches into the depths of his own soul during his famous "Confrontation with the Unconscious" (1913–1930),[2] Jung discovered that there is an intelligent, creative, and life-affirming principle in the human Unconscious that interacts with consciousness and works to further the soul's evolution into integral wholeness. Jung came to call our spiritual journey into wholeness "the individuation process" or realization of "the Self," which is the central archetype or *Imago Dei* (God-image) in the human Unconscious.[3] The activity of this mysterious principle involves a dynamic interaction and dialogue between consciousness and the Unconscious that may be identified with what Jung called "the Transcendent Function."[4] The *Imago Dei* or "Self" corresponds to Christ/Beauty on the Qabalistic Tree of Life.

From my own Christian contemplative perspective, Jung's transcendent-function concept suggests the work of inner redemption (Divine Therapy) Christ does in our soul through the infused gift of *apophatic* contemplation and the consent of Centering Prayer, or any method that invites the grace of God's unconscious presence and action in us. As Thomas Keating explains, receptive methods of prayer or meditation (like Centering Prayer) open us to the energies of the Unconscious and invite the transformative activity of the divine action (Will of Divine Love) to have its way in us, as our consent deepens and evolves into full and free surrender to God's loving Will.[5] The process of receptive contemplation creates a deepening of intimacy in our relationship with God wherein, among other things, the divine action reveals us to our self by bringing into consciousness the dark side of our personality and the toxic residue of unhealed memories, wounds and relationships. This process of gaining new and deepening self-knowledge brings us to true humility via what Thomas Keating has called "the unloading of the Unconscious."[6]

C. G. Jung's confrontation with the Unconscious was a sacred journey into the mysteries of the human soul. Facilitated by his original method of "active imagination" (which gives free play to the Unconscious), and by his discovery of the Transcendent Function, Jung's self-experimentation of inner exploration amounted to a most incredible and spectacular unloading of the Unconscious, which revealed itself to him through a powerful and sometimes overwhelming series of dreams, visions, altered states of consciousness, and intra-psychic spiritual communications. In later life (1957), Jung said of his confrontation with the Unconscious: *The years.... when I pursued the inner images, were the most important time of my life. Everything else is to be derived from this.... My entire life consisted in elaborating what had burst forth from the unconscious and flooded me like an enigmatic stream and threatened to break me.*[7]

Jung's inner odyssey of confrontation with the Unconscious is documented verbally and visually in *The Red Book: Liber Novus*, which, until 2009, was not available to the general public. Though he considered it, Jung was reluctant to publish this most personal work of his. One reason for withholding *The Red Book* from publication may have been that, owing to its subjectively uncritical spiritual and religious contents (as an uncensored revelation of the Unconscious), and owing to the adverse relationship between science and religion in his day, Jung feared *The Red Book* would damage his credibility as a scientist in the eyes of his peers.[8]

The human soul's religious quest is ultimately our search for enduring meaning, value, and fulfillment in this life and beyond. The deeply personal, subjective, and revelatory nature of Jung's experiences and discoveries as recorded in *The Red Book*, which is like an illuminated prophetic manuscript, had to be interpreted and translated into the more objective language and perspective of Jung's voluminous scholarly and theoretical works. Like his prophetic contemporary, Pierre Tielhard de Chardin (see chapter 3), Carl Jung was a pioneer in bridging the early twentieth century's unfriendly abyss between science and religion.

II

In his article, "The Transcendent Function,"[9] which was originally written in 1916, revised in 1953, and not published until 1958, Jung speaks of how the Unconscious naturally resists conscious attitudes, ideas, and actions that are overly one-sided. This resistance is a form of compensation that expresses the human psyche's self-regulating tendency to create balance within itself. The process of unconscious compensation inevitably results in dualistic oppositions and dramatic conflicts between consciousness and the Unconscious; that is, the Unconscious compensates by creating or harboring attitudes, ideas, desires, and actions that contradict and are in direct opposition to those in the conscious mind that are overly one-sided and out of balance with reality.

In this context, and owing to our innate attractions to both Good and Evil (which create our micro-spirituality spectrum), we are thus capable of the widest range of positive and negative attitudes, ideas, desires and actions. The immature ego's conscious denial of this truth pushes our perspective out of balance with reality—so we do not see our self as we actually are. This evokes the compensatory action of the Transcendent Function. Hence, in the relativity of created reality, there's a bright side to every shadow and a shadow side to every light that may darken or illumine the human soul's creative self-expressions in the drama and game of God's Great Adventure. This dualistic principle of opposites in the soul is fundamental to our psychology as evolving human beings and spiritual beings. Becoming truly conscious of it requires the death of our most cherished illusions and does not come easy due to the deep-seated, fear-motivated ego-defense mechanisms and resistance of the insecure false self. It requires repeated acts of faith, courage, and openness to the energies of the Unconscious to see and accept the reality of our complex dual nature.

Conscious awareness of our conflicted dualistic nature evolves over time and brings us to true humility, allowing us to see our self in accordance with reality and the truth of our soul. This is the truth Jesus speaks of in his wisdom saying: *"You will know the truth, and the truth will make you free"* (John 8:32). Accepting and integrating the truth of our soul makes us free to become our true Self. The Transcendent Function operates in service to this truth, to reveal us to our self. Unconscious compensations for one-sided conscious attitudes, ideas, desires, and actions are the first essential step in this process. Thus, self-regulation of the psyche by means of unconscious compensations is an important part of the work of the Transcendent Function, which then seeks to reveal the soul's inner truth of contradictions and conflicts to the conscious mind.

The principle of compensation plays a central role in Jung's Psychology of the Unconscious (as mentioned above), and in Spiritual Psychology as related to Centering Prayer's conceptual background. In the centering-prayer model, the false self's emotional programs for happiness are unconscious attempts to compensate for the felt privations and pain of unmet basic instinctual needs that have been wounded in early life by real or imagined trauma, abuse, or neglect.[10] The sad tragedy of these unconscious programs for compensation lies not only in the suffering, damage, and degradation they create, but in the fatal flaw of their utter futility; that is, in the unhappy fact that they may never truly satisfy us—even in the unlikely event that we somehow do happen to get all they can possibly give us. This is so because the false self and its insatiable happiness programs are conceived in ignorance and fail to recognize or address the true spiritual needs of our soul for love, truth, and freedom.

Inevitable conflicts between conscious and unconscious attitudes, ideas, and desires in the soul are created by the Transcendent Function as it compensates for wounds, one-sidedness, and imbalances in the human personality. These need to be resolved if we're to grow and evolve toward inner wholeness and the realization of our true integral Self. Toward this end, the Transcendent Function works to bring the soul's unresolved unconscious contents to the attention of the conscious mind. It may do this through dreams, fantasies, random thoughts, impulses, creative inspirations, and sudden emotions that burst forth into consciousness. Outer events and relationships may also serve this purpose. Assuming it possesses sufficient ego-strength to do so, the critical issue is always *how* the conscious mind chooses to respond to the invasion of these unconscious contents, which the Transcendent Function brings up into consciousness to heal and integrate the divided personality.

When a weak conscious ego is overwhelmed by negative unconscious contents, then a "psychotic interval" occurs and the personality becomes possessed by its shadowy counterpart. This danger is the rare tragic extreme. Conversely, in the case of stronger egos, if the unconscious contents are denied a hearing, rejected by the conscious mind, and repressed back down into the Unconscious, then the soul's inner rift remains and the individual's growth stagnates in its status quo. This is part of the price we must pay when we're unwilling to face or admit the truth of our soul.

In his transcendent-function article, Jung writes, "those people who are least aware of their unconscious side are the most influenced by it."[11] This telling truth challenges us to honor, respect, listen to, and accept the validity and importance of what the Unconscious communicates to us—even when it's confusing or contradicts our conscious attitudes, desires, and self-image. This does not mean that we capitulate to Evil or violate our commitment to moral/ethical integrity, but that we honor and fulfill that commitment by being willing to face and integrate the full truth of our soul, which includes its shadowy dark side.

To whatever degree our conscious attitude contains negative, unloving elements of Evil and self-deceptions, its repressed unconscious counterpart (shadow) will contain positive bright elements that are good and true. Thus, relations between consciousness and the Unconscious are riddled with paradox as our unconscious shadow is not all evil and our conscious persona is not all good—though we, in our egocentric blindness, may prefer to believe that they are. Such overly one-sided conscious beliefs naturally evoke counter-balancing compensations from the Transcendent Function in the Unconscious, which further complicates and conflicts our psychological reality. Our inner spiritual obstacles are overcome not by denial or by avoiding them, but by humbly and honestly accepting and integrating them. Openness to this truth frees us and transforms our obstacles from foes into allies.

The healing of the oppositions between consciousness and the Unconscious requires bringing our repressed unconscious contents into consciousness, so we may see more deeply into the truth of our soul. This is precisely what we're faced with in the unloading of the unconscious, which results from the consent of Centering Prayer and the secret work of the divine action in us. It's also exactly what happens through the activity of the Transcendent Function wherein contradictions and conflicts between conscious and unconscious attitudes, ideas, desires, and actions are brought up into consciousness. I suggest that the unloading of the Unconscious is produced by the Transcendent Function that, like unloading, is an activity of the *Imago Dei* (God-image) in the soul. In this we may see a confluence of Centering Prayer and Jungian Psychology. Both are in the service of the same noble purpose—the full completion, integration, and awakening of the soul in its true Self or *Imago Dei*—but they use different methods to pursue this aim.

III

Centering Prayer is *apophatic*, receptive, passive, and grounded in consent to and faith in the divine presence and action deep in our soul's Unconscious. Jungian Psychology is *kataphatic*, receptive to the Unconscious, grounded in active work with dreams, fantasies, and symbols using therapeutic dialogue, active imagination, and various forms of creative self-expression to manifest the contents of the Unconscious into consciousness. The method of Centering Prayer is described in the beginning of chapter 5 (pages 85–87). Active imagination is a principle practice in Jungian Psychology. Carl Jung developed this method during his early years of confrontation with the Unconscious, as recorded in *The Red Book*. Jung discovered and practiced active imagination as a dynamic process of interaction between consciousness and the Unconscious using the ancient symbolic language of spontaneous images and fantasies. This allowed him to objectify his unconscious contents via creative self-expression, so that he could consciously acknowledge and relate to them.

Such inner work begins by respecting the Unconscious and taking it seriously, as opposed to consciously ignoring or dismissing it. As we speak to our Unconscious, so does it answer us. Unconscious contents may function as our ally or as our foe, depending on how we relate to or ignore them. The Unconscious has its own special language, which is symbolic, allegorical, metaphorical, and analogous. If we want to communicate well with our Unconscious, we need to learn its unique symbolic language of images. In Centering Prayer, we ignore the images as best we can, letting them all go by like boats floating down our stream of consciousness. In Jungian Psychology, we engage the images as coded messages from our Unconscious. Centering Prayer is *apophatic* (without images). Jungian Psychology is *kataphatic* (with images). This is the fundamental difference between these two complementary methods of working with the Unconscious.

In the *Prefatory Note* to "The Transcendent Function,"[12] Jung writes:

> The method of "active imagination"…, is the most important auxiliary for the production of those contents of the unconscious which lie…, immediately below the threshold of consciousness and, when intensified, are most likely to irrupt spontaneously into the conscious mind. The method, therefore, is not without its dangers and should, if possible, not be employed except under expert supervision.

Marie-Louise von Franz, perhaps Jung's brightest student, writes that "active imagination" is Jung's, "way of dealing with the unconscious," which he taught "to many of his patients." Dr. von Franz then writes, "In principle active imagination consists in suspending the critical faculty and allowing emotions, affects, fantasies, obsessive thoughts or even waking dream-images to come up from the unconscious and in confronting them as if they were objectively present."[13] Any communication from the Unconscious may be used as a starting point for active imagination—whether it comes from a dream, fantasy, emotion, intuition, or anything else of an energetic subjective nature that arises in our consciousness as a result of stimulation from within or from without.

The play of creative fantasy (which allows us to recover some of the spontaneity, creativity, and care-free innocence of childhood), is a key to active imagination. This collaboration between consciousness and the Unconscious, wherein each side plays alternating active and passive roles like two equal partners exchanging the lead in a spontaneous dance, facilitates the Transcendent Function and generates constructive changes and new relationships in the psychodynamics of the Unconscious and its relationship to consciousness. Inner healing and growth are evidenced by new attitudes in the conscious mind that are more in tune with reality and the truth of our soul; that is, constructive active imagination evolves the soul toward growing acceptance of what is, inner peace, wellbeing and higher levels of integration.

There is generally some new composite mediating symbol presented to consciousness by the Unconscious that facilitates inner healing and growth by uniting conflicting opposites on higher levels of integration, harmony, and wholeness. After developing his ideas regarding healing and integration in the psyche, Jung found many confirmatory examples of them in his detailed researches into Hermetic philosophy, Christian Alchemy, Eastern meditation, and mysticism (e.g., Buddhist mandala symbolism and transmuting metals in alchemy).[14] The work of the Transcendent Function in the soul is a movement from duality into non-duality as new life-affirming possibilities are awakened and realized. It is the simple unhindered movement of unconscious contents into consciousness and their welcoming acceptance by the conscious mind that sets the stage for this inner drama of healing and growth in the soul to be played and acted out via the process of active imagination.

Dr. von Franz writes,

An alert, wakeful confrontation with the contents of the unconscious...is the very essence of active imagination. This calls for
an ethical commitment in relation to the manifestations from
within, otherwise one falls prey to the power principle and
the exercise of imagination is destructive both to others and
to the subject.... Fantasies can be objectified by writing them,
by drawing, painting or (rarely) by dancing them. A written
dialogue [between the opposing attitudes of consciousness and
the Unconscious] is the most differentiated form and usually
yields the best results.... Active imagination is the most effective means through which the patient can become independent
of the therapist and learn to stand on his own feet. However, he
must then undertake the inner work on his own, for no one else
can do it for him.[15]

When Dr. von Franz says that active imagination calls for "an ethical commitment" in relation to our unconscious contents, she seems
to be cautioning us that the process holds potential dangers and may
challenge us with some basic good-versus-evil choices regarding illusions and reality.

IV

In both applied Jungian Psychology and daily Centering Prayer practice we are educated through interactions with our Unconscious,
which may speak to us directly or indirectly as we receive and respond
to what confronts us. This education is facilitated by our consciously
consenting to and cooperating with the Transcendent Function and
secret work of God's divine guidance and action in our soul. Centering Prayer and the Transcendent Function both eventually lead to
positive changes in our conscious attitudes and outlook.

In Centering Prayer's Divine Therapy, the healing work takes
place mostly "in secret," in the Unconscious and is typically accompanied by the unloading of unconscious contents. In Jungian Psychology's active-imagination process, the healing takes place in
a two-way dialogue between consciousness and the Unconscious.

This happens as the conscious mind actively plays with and creates upon the symbolic energetic material provided by the Unconscious. We may respond to the Unconscious by means of our attitudes and actions, and through creative fantasy and various forms of self-expression—as mentioned above. When images move energy in the course of constructive active imagination, new configurations of energies and the symbols that contain them are constellated in the Unconscious, creating new conscious attitudes that are not conflicted or delusional but in tune with reality. This is the work of the Transcendent Function.

The consent of Centering Prayer evokes the Transcendent Function on a deeper level, in the hidden Wall of Silence, giving the divine action carte-blanche permission to do whatever needs to be done to free us from our unconscious obstacles and bring us into the fullness of divine union. This happens in the Unconscious as we willingly consent and work to let go of false-self attitudes and desires on the conscious level over time. In Jungian Psychology, the Transcendent Function works in dialogue with consciousness through the Walls of Thoughts and Energy. Unconscious dynamics change via conscious cooperation and consent, causing the unconscious roots of our conscious attitudes and desires to realign themselves with our better angels. In each case, changes in our conscious attitudes and outlook are created by the secret inner work of the Transcendent Function.

Either method requires our willing consent and cooperation. I suggest that the Transcendent Function is the same as the divine action. It operates differently in the two methods of Centering Prayer and active imagination; these two may usefully complement, support, and reinforce each other. In other words, Centering Prayer may add a new dimension and effectiveness to Jungian Psychology, while the perspective and methods of Jungian Psychology may enhance the inner work of Centering Prayer by facilitating the unloading of the Unconscious and help resolve dualistic conflicts and contradictions between our false and true Self.

V

The Transcendent Function's work in the soul may be seen as analogous to the Hegelian dialectic of thesis, antithesis, and synthesis as follows: 1.) The conscious mind's adoption of attitudes, ideas, desires, and actions that are one-sided and out of balance with reality creates a thesis; 2) To compensate for this imbalance, the Transcendent Function creates counter attitudes, ideas, desires, and actions in the Unconscious to form an antithesis; 3) To resolve the resulting conflict and tensions in the soul, the Transcendent Function then works to bring the incongruous unconscious contents into consciousness so that, *if* the conscious mind is open, willing, and cooperates, the conflicting opposites may be united by a new composite integrating symbol. This new symbol, containing the energies of both sides of the conflict, resolves the conflict by integrating its energies, thus creating a healthier, more mature and inclusive attitude, idea, etc. in a new synthesis of intra-psychic wholeness. Such activity by the Transcendent Function integrates and evolves the individual consciousness, bringing it into increasing harmony with reality and the root of true perspective.

This outlines, in very general terms, the complex process of inner healing and transformation that occurs in both Jungian Psychology and Centering Prayer. Each individual case is unique and expresses itself in unique personal symbols; though the general principles or Laws governing the soul's destiny and growth are the same in everyone. The Jungian method requires active conscious participation and engagement in the Walls of Energy and Thoughts; while in Centering Prayer's Divine Therapy, thoughts are disengaged and the inner work of transformation occurs mostly "in secret," in the Unconscious, as the individual rests, consenting to the divine action in the *apophatic* Wall of Silence. In both cases, the work of inner healing and transformation is performed by the divine action (Transcendent Function) with our willing consent, trust, and conscious cooperation.

VI

Jungian Psychology is a vast and fascinating subject. In this chapter, we've only touched upon one important aspect of it (the Transcendent Function and active imagination) in relation to Centering Prayer. There is need for much more investigation and research. In a 1954 letter, Jung wrote regarding the Transcendent Function:

> To find the answer.... we can but trust to our mental powers on the one hand and on the other to the functioning of the unconscious, that spirit which we cannot control. It can only be hoped that it is a "holy" spirit. The cooperation of conscious reasoning with the data of the unconscious is called the "transcendent function."...This function progressively unites the opposites. Psychotherapy makes use of it to heal neurotic dissociations, but this function had already served as the basis of Hermetic philosophy for seventeen centuries. Besides this, it is a natural and spontaneous phenomenon, part of the process of individuation. Psychology has no proof that this process does not unfold itself at the instigation of God's will.
>
> The Holy Spirit will manifest himself in any case in the psychic sphere of man and will be presented as a psychic experience. He thus becomes the object of empirical psychology, which he will need in order to translate his symbolism into the possibilities of this world. Since his intention is the incarnation, that is, the realization of the divine being in human life, he cannot be a light which the darkness comprehendeth not.... The opposites are kept in balance, and so the kingdom of Christ is followed by that of Antichrist. In the circumstances the Holy Spirit, the third form of God, becomes of extreme importance, for it is thanks to him that the man of good will is drawn toward the divine drama and mingled in it, and the Spirit **is one**. In him the opposites are separated no longer.[16]

It is the Will of Divine Love that unites them.

7

Working with the Unconscious

Seven Psycho-Spiritual Practices

I

Centering Prayer, as taught by Thomas Keating and Contemplative Outreach, is a method par excellence for working with the Unconscious, developing intimacy with God and evolving toward integral wholeness in our true Self. Jungian active imagination is another, complementary method for relating to our unconscious contents, engaging the Transcendent Function (divine action), and facilitating inner healing through the union of conflicting opposites in our soul. In addition to these primary methods, there are several other psychospiritual practices that may serve to promote inner freedom, spiritual growth, and consciousness evolution. Among these are: using an active prayer sentence; inner work (self-inquiry and self-observation) and the way of the Cross, the Welcoming Prayer, the Five-Step Forgiveness Process, work with dreams, the creative arts, and the "Just Noticing" practice. We'll focus on these in this chapter:

II

The active prayer sentence (traditionally, *Guard of the Heart*), comes out of the ancient Judeo-Christian Tradition, from the days when worshippers would repeat simple words or phrases from the Scriptures to themselves as they went through the activities of their daily lives. It is a *kataphatic* prayer practice involving a lot of repetition, so that, over time, the active prayer phrase gradually works its way into the subconscious mind and eventually begins to automatically repeat itself. The Jesus Prayer, "Lord Jesus Christ, Son of the Living God, have mercy on me, a sinner," is a well-known example of active prayer practice, as are "O God, come to my assistance, O Lord, make haste to help me" and "God is love."[1]

The active prayer phrase is repeated in free moments when whatever we're doing does not require all of our attention. It may be used before falling asleep at night, before getting out of bed in the morning, or whenever we're "waiting" or doing something that's relatively automatic during the day. It helps to make our time more productive on a spiritual level in at least two ways: 1) Active prayer practice is a way of praying relatively continually because it helps us to live daily life in relation to God on a conscious level, subtly reminding us of God's presence. This helps to keep us connected to our spiritual center and values in a variety of circumstances.

2) In addition to supporting our connection to God in daily life, using an active prayer sentence may serve as a buffer to help us cope with inner and outer situations that challenge our inner poise and peace by distracting, irritating, or tempting us to act out of false-self emotions. This typically happens when one of our emotional programs for happiness is either frustrated or gratified.[2] The false self's emotional happiness programs are powerful habits of self-centered desire rooted in the soul's unconscious instinctual energy centers in the Foundation Sphere on the Tree of Life. These happiness programs are compensatory distortions and exaggerations of our unmet or wounded basic instinctual needs for security/survival/safety, sensation/pleasure, affection/esteem/approval, power/control, and intimacy/belonging. They all have a variety of afflictive emotions attached to them that are activated when emotional happiness programs are either frustrated or gratified. Some common examples of these afflictive emotions are: grief; pride; anger; hatred; envy; jealousy; greed; lust; worry-doubt feelings of insecurity, fear, guilt, and anxiety; impatience; boredom; apathy; loneliness; and depression.

The active prayer sentence offers a simple way of coping with the false self's emotional happiness programs and their related afflictive emotions whenever these come up into consciousness to adversely impact or pleasantly distract our state of mind. The active prayer is not meant to be used to deny or repress afflictive emotions, which actually makes them worse, but as a positive means to keep our self from being pushed off balance, controlled by afflictive emotions and acting them out in ways that we will later regret. Afflictive emotions of the false self come from the root of false perspective at the dark end of our micro-spirituality spectrum, distorting our immediate view of reality and of what's really important to us.

Afflictive emotions invading consciousness are like an attack of demons, our personal demons. Reverting to an established active prayer sentence when afflictive emotions arise helps us to maintain our inner spiritual poise and balance, which connects us to our root of true perspective within. This gives us a space of freedom in which to consciously choose what to do with whatever afflictive emotions we're feeling—as opposed to unconsciously identifying with them, giving in to them, mindlessly acting them out and allowing afflictive emotions to dominate consciousness and the spirit in which we act.

Individual psycho-spiritual circumstances regarding vulnerability to afflictive emotions may differ widely from one person to another. Some souls are subject to outbursts of uncontrollable anger, unseemly urges, or bouts of debilitating depression, while others are more mildly afflicted by self-contained automatic reactions, such as irritating impatience, self-indulgent fantasies, or controllable anger. In differing cases, the active prayer sentence needs to be used differently, relative to the severity and potential danger of afflictive emotions. In more severe cases, the active prayer phrase may be used to sidestep or deflect an afflictive emotion, to prevent the individual from being overtaken by the emotion and acting it out in a harmful way. Such stopgap measures serve to circumvent destructive reactions like physical violence or severe verbal abuse directed toward another person. In such cases, the person is not yet ready or spiritually strong enough to consciously encounter her or his afflictive emotions without danger to self or others.

In less severe cases, an individual may safely allow oneself to experience more fully an afflictive emotion without being overpowered by it and compelled to mindlessly act it out. The afflictive emotion is consciously recognized, felt, and then denied outer expression as one endures its attack, focusing on God's abiding, loving presence by repeating the active prayer phrase—thus affirming one's commitment to inner peace, patience, forgiveness, and self-restraint in solidarity with Jesus on the Cross. This serves to strengthen the soul in virtue while depriving the afflictive emotion and its source in the Unconscious of fresh energy, affirmation, and reinforcement. The same thing happens in the more severe cases of dangerous afflictive emotions, but to a lesser degree. Whenever we avoid acting out an afflictive emotion or any habit, we deprive it of energy—thereby weakening its hold on us. This is a primary function of the active prayer sentence.

III

Various versions of inner work involving self-inquiry and self-observation may be found in sacred and secular traditions throughout the world. For example, the Delphic Oracle's Temple inscription: *know thyself*, and the famous statement: *the unexamined life isn't worth living* (attributed to Socrates), are calls to self-inquiry and self-observation from the wisdom of ancient Greece. The Buddhist practice of *mindfulness* is another example, as are the *examination of conscience* and *Way of the Cross* in Christianity. Self-inquiry and self-observation serve to bring habitual behavior patterns that have become automatic and unconscious up into consciousness, where they may be reflected upon and evaluated.

Inner work begins by taking honest stock of the situation in which we find ourselves. This is a continuing process of self-inquiry and self-observation that progresses over time, going deeper and deeper into increasingly more subtle levels of the soul. Self-inquiry involves looking deeply into our self and searching out honest answers to questions such as: *Who am I? What am I? What do I really want?* Self-inquiry is best done in the presence of our conscience or "better angels." The conscience is an intuitive inner voice of divine guidance and wisdom God has placed in each soul. It is the advocate for our spiritual growth in love and knows in advance the results of each choice we consider acting upon. We get in touch with our conscience by listening inside our self for its gentle communication of suggestions, which we are always free to ignore or follow.

Self-observation practice accompanies and complements self-inquiry by impartially witnessing and noting what we repeatedly do in daily life, so we may become more consciously aware of our automatic patterns of thought, feeling, speech, desire, and action. Self-observation does not judge our self or our behavior. It simply collects our behavioral data by objectively observing and noting it, continually taking an inventory of our habits, which may include judging our self or others. The practice of self-observation takes us a step back from the less conscious perspectives of personal ego-involvement and identification with our roles in the drama and game of God's Great Adventure. This gives us new opportunities for clarity and detachment in viewing our self, our life, our motivations, and desires.

As we inventory our personal habits of thought, feeling, and so on, perhaps writing them down on a list, the next step in self-observation is to discover the immediate and longer-term results that particular habits create for us. This further step of self-observation allows us to become consciously aware of the cause/effect relationships between particular habits and their consequent outcomes. Given this new information, we may then inquire as to whether or not each of our automatic habit patterns is serving us well; that is, creating results that we want in our life? In this way, we may become more self-aware and separate out those habits that express our spiritual values and serve us well versus those habit patterns that are making our life worse. As we research our soul in this way and begin to identify our healthy versus our unhealthy habit patterns, we may then enter onto the way of the Cross, which is a process of dying to our false self and eliminating its destructive habit patterns in solidarity with Jesus Christ.[3]

Chief among habits that make our life worse are the false self's emotional programs for happiness and the afflictive emotions attached to them. These are powerful habit patterns that become automatic and unconscious in the human soul from early life. The strength of these addictive happiness programs and their accompanying afflictive emotions is relative to the severity of the soul's wounding and the amount of energy built up within and around them in the Unconscious. Our unhealed emotional wounds and self-defeating habits (false happiness programs) *are* our personal demons, which we have knowingly or unknowingly created. Hence, we are responsible for them, and for all we create in the four lower Spheres on the Tree of Life where Good and Evil vie for dominion (see diagram on page 7).[4] Our power and need to create are natural consequences of being created in God's image and likeness (Gen. 1:26–27).

All our habits, whether good or bad, are created by us and strengthened by repetition, gradually becoming automatic unconscious response patterns in the soul that, unbeknownst to us, take on a life and consciousness of their own inside us. Our habits are our personal angelic or demonic creations, depending on their spiritual qualities and the results they create in our life. Human habits live in our soul and cannot generate their own energy, as we can through connection to the divine indwelling within us. Thus, our habits are dependent on us (as we are dependent on God) and nourished by the energy that we give them. The more energy we give to a particular habit, through more and more repetition and emotional investment, the stronger it becomes.

When a bad habit becomes stronger than our will to resist it, then we have a serious personal problem threatening our freedom; an unhealthy addiction that's bound to create gradual or sudden destruction and misery in our life. I define an addiction as any habitual pattern of behavior that we cannot stop repeating, whether we want to stop or not. Under this definition, there are both healthy and unhealthy addictions. Healthy addictions are related to meeting our legitimate basic instinctual needs for survival, pleasure, esteem, power, etc. These needs are life affirming when honored and expressed appropriately. Unhealthy addictions are related to the misuse, abuse, denial, overindulgence, or perversion of our basic instinctual needs, which then become life-negating and destructive demonic habits in the soul. The various ways in which people may relate to food, sex, power, and various forms of ego-gratifying pleasure give us numerous examples of healthy versus unhealthy addictions—each of which, as a conscious autonomous complex in the soul, has its own innate survival drive, appetite, and felt-need for energy to sustain it.

In worst-case scenarios, individuals find themselves in the grip of self-defeating unhealthy habit patterns that they can't control. It may be a chemical dependency like drug or alcohol addiction, food abuse, compulsive gambling or sexual promiscuity, emotional dependency or instability, patterns of negative self-talk, lying, stealing, cheating, a need to dominate, manipulate or bully others, addiction to cheap thrills and risk-taking. Or it may be something subtler and less obvious. Whatever the case may be, and it's often a combination of unhealthy addictions, the bad habits running and ruining a person's life, and important relationships are out of control. The hapless individual suffers and feels powerless to change the situation for the better. This is a condition of psycho-spiritual slavery, traditionally called *bondage to sin*. Demonic habits do not respect the integrity of their creator host's free will, but care only for the continuing and perhaps unlimited gratification of their immediate self-centered desire. So what's to be done? How to get free from psycho-spiritual bondage to demonic habit patterns? How to make and sustain meaningful healthy change in one's life? This is a critical, dramatic, and universal question of the human condition. Freedom is always possible, if we're willing to work for it.

The basic solution is this: having practiced self-inquiry and self-observation to become consciously aware of our demonic habit patterns (which are rooted in the Unconscious), we need to weaken them by depriving them of energy. Two effective ways of doing this are 1) to stop feeding them energy by indulging or repeating them and 2) to get them to expend their energy, which inevitably happens when we resist them and they attack us with afflictive emotions to bully us into submission to their self-centered will. The stubborn and disappointing difficulty arises when, wanting to resist an adversarial demon-habit, we discover that we're powerless to do so by relying on our own efforts and resources because, unfortunately, the personal demon we've created is actually stronger than our will to resist it. At this point, one may feel helpless, hopeless, discouraged, and depressed.

However, this discouraging defeat need not be the end of our story here in the drama and game of God's Adventure. We simply need to humbly recognize that we need help to overcome our self-created adversary. Fortunately, human and divine help are readily available from without and from within, if we're willing to confess our weakness and ask for help. Outwardly, we may seek help from such sources as friends, loved ones, professional addiction counselors, psychotherapists, twelve-step programs, or religious or spiritual guidance.

Humanly assisted psycho-spiritual methods and techniques for dealing with stubborn unwanted habits may range from treating surface symptoms, with, say, behavior modification techniques or hypnosis, to pursuing a symptom's underlying unconscious cause with methods that indirectly address the Unconscious. We may work with the Unconscious only indirectly because it is, by definition, unconscious and therefore unavailable to direct conscious communication or manipulation. We have to work *with* the Unconscious, not upon it. Hence, the Jungian approach of dialogue with the Unconscious—via symbolic methods like active imagination, dream analysis, conscious visualizations, and ritual activities relating to the Unconscious—is effective and educational, in the sense of drawing forth from within the wisdom of the Unconscious. This correlates to contents of the Wall of Energy in the soul becoming part of the Wall of Thoughts, once they've become objectified and conscious.

IV

The complementary alternative to seeking outer help with unhealthy addictive habits through human or other agencies—like Nature—is seeking the divine help that's available within the soul. We may do this through prayer and engaging a working intimate partnership with Christ. This brings us to the Way of the Cross, which implements Jesus' teaching that to be his disciple, we must deny our false self, take up our Cross and follow him (Matt. 10:38 and 16:24). The way of the Cross is our symbolic, allegorical participation in the Paschal Mystery and Cross of Christ.

We take up our Cross whenever, in the context of our intimate relationship with God, we accept to carry the unavoidable burdens, pain, difficulties, and challenges that life brings us. The Way of the Cross is easily misunderstood, especially by non-Christians. It's not meant to be perverted into a path of self-defeating masochism or meaningless suffering. Any path of life-negating asceticism or self-righteous self-denial (like the heresy of Jansenism) is Evil's counterfeit imitation of the true Way of the Cross, which is a path to inner healing, peace, and liberation in the Love of Christ. The suffering aspect of the Cross is a means to the most positive spiritual end, and not an end in itself. The aim or end of the Way of the Cross is inner resurrection and rebirth in Christ.

The Way of the Cross allows us to work in partnership with Christ in the Unconscious. It calls for humility, trust, and faith on our part, and willingness to embrace the Cross of Christ, which, at first glance, is definitely not appealing to us, just as it was not appealing to Jesus in the garden of Gethsemane (Matt. 26:36–46). The Cross is a powerful symbol of transformation, especially in the context of the Paschal Mystery in which all followers of Jesus are called to allegorically participate in the inner life of our souls. That is, we are called to undergo the death and rebirth process of our false self transforming into our true Self as symbolized by Christ's death on the Cross, his descent into hell (the dark, horrific aspect of the Unconscious), and his triumphal resurrection into eternal life on Easter morning. This is not a one-time event, but a life-long, cyclical, repeating pattern of evolving psycho-spiritual integration in the true center of our being.

So how may we follow the way of the Cross? Thomas Keating has suggested that in Centering Prayer practice, during times of dryness, boredom, unloading the Unconscious, or the Dark Nights, we may picture our self seated on the Cross with Jesus. This is a practical, workable way of embracing the Way of the Cross and the Cross of Christ. While we're enduring difficulties in prayer, experiencing the "spiritual desert," the Holy Spirit is secretly at work in the Unconscious, purifying, healing, and transforming the soul. Since we can't normally see this happening, we are called by faith to trust that it is happening; not on our terms but on God's terms and in God's time. This patient, humble discipline in Centering Prayer is a loving act of surrender to the Will of Divine Love.

In the same way, we may practice the Way of the Cross when experiencing and resisting the pull of unhealthy demonic habits and the attacks of their afflictive emotions. This is particularly important when we're contending with the attacks of personal demons that are stronger than we are. We may draw strength from the Spirit of Christ in solidarity with him on the Cross. We'll still suffer the pains of withdrawal from the self-destructive addictions of our bad habits, unhealed wounds, and emotional happiness programs, paying the purifying price for our errors and faulty creations. However, this suffering is not meaningless but healing and redemptive.

Whenever we refuse to indulge our unhealthy demonic habits, we deprive them of fresh energy, which gradually weakens their hold on us. When our demons attack with afflictive emotions, trying to bully and force us into indulging their self-centered desires, they expend a lot more of the energy we've built up within them. If we hold firm to the Cross of refusal in solidarity with Jesus, who gives us the strength we need to endure this psycho-spiritual torture inflicted by our self-created demons; this weakens them further. The pain of withdrawal from toxic addictive habits may seem endless and is hard to endure, but it only lasts so long, like the timed rounds of a boxing match.

Eventually it passes, and when it does, though we may feel emotionally beaten, bruised and tired, our demonic adversary will have lost the round and grown weaker in energy, will, and power—while we will actually have grown a bit stronger in relation to it. Eventually, after many hard-fought and long-suffered rounds, the bad habit that was stronger than our will to resist it will be stronger no longer. It then becomes easier to habitually resist this demon of our own making, which weakens out in its greed as we continue to refuse it. This liberating inner work, which we cannot accomplish on our own as a separate self, is the freedom fruit of self-inquiry, self-observation and embracing the Cross of Christ, which strengthens and supports us in our struggle against the foe.

Though weakened by energy starvation, however, the personal demon of our deadly bad habit is not yet fully vanquished. Weakened by repeated refusals and suppressed by the conscious mind, a demonic habit that was stronger than our will to resist it remains active and aware in the Unconscious, so long as it has energy and life within it. It lies in wait inside us for an occasion of the requisite symbolic imagery in our outer life and relationships to "push a psycho-spiritual button" in the Unconscious and call its automatic pattern up into action and outer expression. Whenever this happens, a sudden impulse to spontaneously repeat the demonic habit pattern will suddenly arise in consciousness, and we will be challenged with a point of immediate choice as to whether or not we give in to this impulse. If we do give in, we feed our personal demon energy and it begins to grow stronger again. If we're consciously aware enough to recognize it before automatically following the impulse, and we refuse it, then the bad habit in question loses energy and grows weaker still. It may try attacking us with afflictive emotions, but this will only further weaken it, so long as we don't give in to the afflictive emotions' repulsive negativity or attractive lure.

The healthy habits of self-inquiry and self-observation give us the presence of mind to spot the reactive impulses of our unconscious demonic habits; and when we do, we have opportunities to "take up our Cross" and deprive them of energy. As we continue in this way, eventually our demonic foes will become drained of all their energy and be relatively powerless to influence us; but they won't be gone from our life yet. Unconscious habit patterns exist as energy-containing forms or structures in the subtle astral matter of the soul's Foundation Sphere on its microcosmic Tree of Life. In order for bad demonic habits to be completely eliminated and gone, not only must they be emptied of energy, but the subtle astral forms or patterned symbolic structures that define them and hold their energy must be destroyed as well. This is the work of the Holy Spirit or divine action deep in our soul.

How this works is illustrated by the analogy of a well-trained opera singer shattering an empty crystal wine glass with the vibratory power of her soprano voice. The opera singer represents the Holy Spirit and the empty crystal wine glass corresponds to the patterned, energy-containing astral form of a demonic habit. The wine that is poured into the wine glass represents the energy that gives life and strength to a habit. As long as there is wine in the glass, the opera singer cannot shatter it because the wine gives its molecular structure stability and support. It's only when the glass is empty that it may be shattered by the sustained requisite sound vibrations.

How does this work? The singer (Holy Spirit) vibrates her voice at a frequency that matches and unites with the vibratory frequency of the crystal molecules in the wine glass. After uniting with them, she raises the pitch of her voice, thereby raising the vibratory frequency of the crystal molecules beyond the range of their ability to hold together, and the wine glass explodes into many disintegrated pieces. This is what the divine action does, with our willing consent, to the demonic habit patterns in our soul, once they're fully drained of the energy we've given them. This is how a person's self-created demonic habit patterns in the soul may be vanquished and utterly destroyed. Once the process is completed, we are permanently free from an unwanted unconscious habit and its ability to influence us; unless we choose to re-create and resurrect the habit by repeating it over and over again, which is unlikely, since we've learned through bitter experience that it does not give us what we want in our life and soul.

The inner work of self-inquiry, self-observation, and the Way of the Cross as discussed above may be effectively facilitated by the use of an active prayer sentence. Using an active prayer sentence helps us to maintain a conscious connection to God and our spiritual values. It reminds us of our better intentions, spiritual priorities, and higher values in the face of contrary temptations, afflictive emotions, and urges of demonic habits that may suddenly manifest into consciousness—given the presence of certain triggering events and the requisite evocative symbolism in our outer life and relationships. Whenever we are resisting bad habits and the attacks of their afflictive emotions, repeating an active prayer sentence helps us to focus in solidarity with Jesus on the Cross of Christ and, with God's help, to endure the sufferings of withdrawal from unhealthy addictions that work to overpower us from both the spiritual and physiological levels of our being.

Physiologically, there are compelling biochemical and neurologic triggers to all addictive habits and their urges. Addictive habits may originate on either the physical or psycho-spiritual level of the human organism. Chemical reactions and the repeated, automatic use of neural pathways in the brain and nervous system constitute the psycho-biology of both healthy and unhealthy addictive habits. The unhealthy ones may be treated by chemical means, such as psychiatric drugs, dietary changes, and avoiding situations, people, and chemical substances (e.g., alcohol or drugs) that tend to trigger our unwanted demonic habits. They may also be treated by redirecting a person's attention, will, and energy (e.g., physical exercise, self-inquiry, self-observation, the Way of the Cross, and using an active prayer phrase). Since there's a two-way, reciprocal relationship between physiology and psychology in human ground (the physical Kingdom Sphere and Personality/Astral Triad on the Tree of Life), these two types of therapeutic methods (physical and spiritual) are not mutually exclusive and may be used effectively in tandem.[5]

Initially, self-inquiry asks and answers in the soul: What do I really care about? What's genuinely important to me? Self-observation is initially done from an objective "witnessing consciousness" that is non-judgmental. The purpose of impartiality in self-observation is to seek objective facts in our behavior without being influenced by any habitual unconscious biases. Once we've clearly determined what we really care about, what's most important to us (e.g., our higher spiritual values), then we may begin to observe and evaluate our habitual patterns of thought, feeling, speech, desire, and action from that perspective. Ideally, we want to practice self-inquiry and self-observation from the perspective of our spiritual values (once we're clear about what those are), our conscience, and in detachment from the agendas of the false-self system. We continue practicing self-inquiry and self-observation while we're practicing the Way of the Cross, which will gradually bring us to inner resurrection and our divine inheritance.

The treasure of our divine inheritance and Will of Divine Love are for each of us to discover in the solitude and privacy of our own inner life and intimate relationship with God. This is where the real action always is in the drama and game of our spiritual journey. In other words, wherever you are now is where the real action is, because wherever you are God is within and around you. We need to find the true center within our self, withdraw all of our unconscious projections, both negative and positive, from other people, God, and the world around us. Only then may we see clearly what is as it is. This means we need to transcend the blinders and prejudices of our cultural conditioning, as well as those of our emotional happiness programs and false self. We transcend these things by becoming conscious of them and how they influence us. The inner work of self-inquiry and self-observation may help us to do this; and so may the Welcoming Prayer of freely facing and fully experiencing whatever manifests in our consciousness.

V

The way of the Cross may be followed via Centering Prayer practice, working with an active prayer sentence, the previously described inner work of self-inquiry and self-observation, the Five-Step Forgiveness Process, and by practicing the Welcoming Prayer. The Welcoming Prayer is a deeply focused practice for working directly with the psycho-spiritual energy and unconscious contents that come up in daily life, personal relationships, or dreams. This prayer greatly facilitates unloading the Unconscious and has been called "consent on the go."[6] Mary Mrozowski (1923–1993) created the Welcoming Prayer practice, which has been nuanced and refined over the years. I was fortunate to meet Mary and learn the Welcoming Prayer practice (originally called "Open Mind, Open Heart Practice") from her at a training retreat for service to Contemplative Outreach in Amarillo, Texas, in 1992. This practice has three basic steps and requires the use of more conscious effort than does using an active prayer sentence. With repeated practice, however, it becomes habitual and requires appreciably less and less time and conscious effort.

Thomas Keating has noted that our physical body "is the warehouse of the unconscious," meaning that our entire life history and unresolved emotional issues are stored in the physical body. Welcoming Prayer is an incarnational psycho-spiritual practice where "the issues are in the tissues." Hence, practicing the Welcoming Prayer involves carefully noticing what's going on in our physical body in conjunction with our thoughts and feelings as we work its three steps. When welcoming intense emotions and major unloading, these steps may require time and repetition to complete.

They are: 1) Focus on, feel, and sink fully into whatever striking feeling (e.g., afflictive emotion) or unconscious content comes up into consciousness (noticing where it's grounded in your physical body); 2) Welcome this experience and God's presence in it, allowing it to intensify and fill your consciousness, so that you become one with the experience; and 3) Release or let go of the experience's inner source, repeating: "I let go of the desire for security, affection, control. I let go of the desire to change what I am experiencing." This prayer is an act of surrender. It's an exercise in opening to and accepting, without reservation, God's presence, action, and the immediate truth of our soul (whatever it may be) in the present moment. We may practice the Welcoming Prayer in relation to positive, pleasurable experiences as well as in relation to unloading experiences that are unpleasant, disturbing, and not wanted by the conscious ego or false self.[7]

Initially, practicing the Welcoming Prayer is counterintuitive and somewhat paradoxical, since it usually involves welcoming what we don't consciously want. It may also involve welcoming and releasing what we do want (so we won't become overly ego-attached or addicted to our self-centered desires). Welcoming Prayer works against the patterns of our established unconscious habits of attachment, aversion, denial, repression, and avoidance of personal demons; that is, the rejected shadowy side of our personality that holds the hunger, pain, fear, and rage of our unhealed emotional wounds, self-centered happiness programs, afflictive emotions, and the split-off parts of our self that we've rejected out of shame, guilt, fear, insecurity, and so on. With the Welcoming Prayer, we consciously open the secret door in our soul to all the unconscious contents within us that need to be unloaded, healed, transformed, and integrated into the wholeness of our conscious self in God. Welcoming Prayer is thus a most practical and powerful way of working on our deepest unconscious issues in partnership with Christ and cooperation with the Transcendent Function (divine action).

This prayer accelerates the process of our inner cleansing, healing, and renewal in the life of Christ. It's a very real way of "taking up our Cross and following Jesus" to the Cross of our false self's gradual psycho-spiritual death and rebirth into our true Self through the grace of inner resurrection. This process frees the soul from its subjection to afflictive emotions, false happiness programs, and the blindness of over-identification with cultural conditioning and the separate-self sense. As we are open to this work, the divine action responds with opportunities. So how does it work?

Ultimately, it works through our growing surrender to the Will of Divine Love. However, before we come to the point of actual surrender to the Will of Divine Love, there are several passages of inner transition we may need to negotiate. These involve the reformation and renewal of the many and conflicting habit patterns that make up our personality construction. The process of rebuilding and renewal in the soul is, of course, the secret work of the divine action in us. This work never violates our relative free will and thus requires our willing cooperation, consent, and actively doing our part. Using the Welcoming Prayer, in conjunction with daily Centering Prayer practice, is an effective way of doing our part.

Doing the Welcoming Prayer draws energy out of the unconscious energy centers (demons or unhealthy addictive habit patterns) that power the false-self system. It involves repeated acts of willingness to see and experience the truth of our soul; that is, willingness to face and feel what's going on inside us on all levels: physical, vital, emotional, mental, psychic, social, and spiritual. We get beyond our afflictive emotions and false-self happiness programs not by avoiding, denying or going around them, but by allowing our self to go straight into and through them. This is the basic discipline of the Welcoming Prayer. As we welcome and embrace our afflictive emotions and other false-self impulses, without acting on them and thus feeding energy into their source in the Unconscious, their energy dissipates and their power to influence us gradually weakens.

Welcoming what is unwelcome to our conscious ego is the essential counterintuitive aspect of this prayer that challenges us to openly accept what we feel strongly inclined to reject. Our inclination to reject comes from anxiety and unwillingness to re-experience repressed unconscious contents in the soul. As Mary Mrozowski put it, Welcoming Prayer is a way of reclaiming the lost, wounded parts of our soul that we've rejected and denied. It's based on the principle that *the truth will make you free* (John 8:32) and involves working progressively through our reactions down into their source in the Unconscious; that is, the emotional happiness programs whose frustrations or gratifications give rise to the various negative or positive afflictive emotions.

Welcoming Prayer also exemplifies the paradoxical principle in psychotherapy that *you have to get worse <u>before</u> you can get better.* This relates directly to the unloading of the Unconscious wherein the hidden causes of unhealthy false-self symptoms need to come up and pass through consciousness *before* they may be fully evacuated, released, and resolved. Hence, symptoms (e.g., afflictive emotions) will intensify and we'll feel worse before we overcome them and become permanently better. This is all part of the Divine Therapy and the Cross of healing.

The mere event of the divine action or Transcendent Function bringing *any* unconscious content up into consciousness, and our taking responsible ownership of it as part of the truth of our soul, automatically changes it and frees us from its previously unknown influence. This empowers us to make a free-choice conscious decision as to what to do with it—to say "yes" or "no" to it. We accept the reality of its presence in us and then freely choose how to respond on the basis of what we really care about.

Hence, Welcoming Prayer involves welcoming everything that's within us (including our shadow), as well as welcoming our automatic false-self reactions to what comes to us from without through other people, events, and situations. The letting go litany in step three of the Welcoming Prayer ("I let go of the desire for security, affection, control; I let go of the desire to change what I am experiencing"), serves to remind and program our personal subconscious with the suggestion that we do not need or really want the false-self desires (emotional happiness programs) that are the source of our afflictive emotions and misguided urges.

Whenever emotional happiness programs are frustrated or gratified, automatic response patterns are activated in the Unconscious, and we experience negative or positive afflictive emotions that come from the root of false perspective in our soul, throwing us off balance and out of touch with our inner spiritual center. Our ego becomes inflated or deflated by an afflictive emotion and we're tempted to act out of our false self under the influence of one or more of its childish happiness programs. If, rather than avoiding or mindlessly acting out some unwanted thought, memory, bodily sensation, urge, or afflictive emotion that comes up into consciousness, we engage the Welcoming Prayer, we deprive its unconscious source of fresh energy. Continuing in this way helps to dismantle the obstacles of the false-self system and allows us to increasingly live our life more consciously and freely in relation to God and what we truly care about.

VI

The Welcoming Prayer is a proactive form of self-inquiry and self-observation that allows us to get in touch with and fully experience our inner feelings, impulses, and desires. In releasing the energy of afflictive emotions and self-centered desires, the Welcoming Prayer, with God's help, helps us to work through and change our inner obstacles and the attitudes that reinforce them. In cases where we harbor anger, hatred, resentment, and desires for revenge against others who have hurt or wronged us, or against our self for any reason, we cannot become free of these obstacles and toxic emotions simply by welcoming them. We need to go through the healing process of forgiveness.

In instances of minor daily-life irritations, it may be possible to let go of petty resentments and forgive on the conscious level alone—perhaps by engaging the Welcoming Prayer. In more serious cases of deeper wounds, however, the healing process of forgiveness requires a thorough working through and completion in the Unconscious, as well as on the conscious level. This is a process of deep healing in the soul that we cannot accomplish by our self on the conscious level because the Unconscious remembers everything that the conscious mind forgets or represses, and unconscious contents have a will and way of their own.

Until, by God's grace, we're able to truly forgive the pain and hurt of our unhealed wounds, both consciously and unconsciously, we shall continue to carry a Cross of inner division in our soul. We shall continue experiencing repeatedly the toxic afflictive emotions and other negative fruits of our bitter inner grudges and unhealed wounds. If we practice the Welcoming Prayer without forgiving the inner cause of afflictive emotions, we'll have to keep welcoming again and again the same unresolved unconscious contents that come up from our refusal to forgive. In other words, thorough healing in the soul requires complete forgiveness.[8] This kind of deep forgiveness comes over time as a gift of the divine action or Transcendent Function in conjunction with our willing consent and cooperation.

The practice of forgiveness is central to Jesus' original and radical teaching that we "love one another" (John 15:17). Though it's truly in our best spiritual interests to forgive, authentic forgiveness is actually an expression of unselfish love and compassion. It's a movement from duality (where we may have good reason not to forgive), into non-duality (where Divine Love transcends all differences). This transcendence of differences in the unity of Divine Love gives rise to the precious root of true perspective in the soul's micro-spiritual spectrum of free-will choices. *As Love determines Justice, so does Will determine Destiny.* When we choose to forgive, we create peace and harmony in our soul. When we refuse to forgive, we create division and disturbance. Consciously or unconsciously holding onto grudges and desires for revenge involves harboring toxic negative emotions. Such negative emotions, festering in the Unconscious, poison the soul and disturb our peace of mind.

Whenever we recite *The Lord's Prayer*, we ask God to forgive us in the same way that we forgive others who may offend or do us wrong. This is an implicit commitment to practice forgiveness in the face of Evil and all wrongdoing we see in our personal life and in the world at large. In the face of extreme atrocities, betrayals, injustice, and malicious evil actions, it's as difficult to humanly forgive the perpetrators as it is to love them. On the dualistic human level of separate-self consciousness, it may well be as impossible to forgive the perpetrators of Evil as it is to condone what they do. True forgiveness, however, never means condoning, ignoring, or forgetting what is evil and wrong. Forgiveness occurs on the spiritual level and involves remembering the truth, accepting what has actually happened as part of the past, and coming to peace with it so we may let it go, place it in the past (where it belongs), and not allow it to poison our peace of mind and sanity in the present. Hence, forgiveness is a process of liberation from the wounds of history and their negative consequences.

The practical question here is: How do we come to forgiveness? There are various approaches to this challenge.[9] Most involve working with memory, creative visualization, and the soul's inherent capacities for prayer, love, and compassion. The Five-Step Forgiveness Process presented here is based on a book by William Meninger, *The Process of Forgiveness*, and on a procedure I learned from a spiritually gifted woman, Dollaine Flohr, who studied and practiced *A Course in Miracles*.

Like Centering Prayer, the Forgiveness Process works in the Unconscious to heal and free us from the burdens of obstacles we carry inside us. To complete this five-step process, we need to repeat it many times over a period of weeks, months, or longer. It is a work the Holy Spirit does in us with our cooperation and consent. It's possible for individuals to get stuck and unconsciously remain in any of the five steps, especially when they're not consciously aware of these steps and how to work through them. These steps are similar to the dying/grieving process first identified by Elizabeth Kubler-Ross in the 1960s.[10]

Instructions for the five steps are as follows:

1. Claiming your hurt: Remember as much as you can about what happened to you. Allow yourself to feel the pain, anger, and all connected to it. Repeat this daily until it's only a memory and no more hurt remains. Do not minimize or deny your feelings, honor them, welcome them, and live them. Take notice of where the feelings of your hurt reside in your physical body. Focus and sink into them, using the Welcoming Prayer to fully experience them. Remember, the people who hurt you were acting out of their own unhealed pain.

2. Dealing with self-blame and guilt: Allow yourself to feel any guilt you have in reaction to the hurt you've experienced. Know this was not your fault; forgive yourself. You did not deserve it. We often unconsciously blame ourselves for bad things that happen to us. This is especially true regarding wounds, neglect, and abuse suffered in early life and childhood. Use the Welcoming Prayer to fully experience any conscious or unconscious feelings of self-blame or guilt you may be carrying. Go on repeating this for days, weeks, months, or longer, until no more self-blame or guilt remain. Know that whatever was done to you was someone else's choice and not your fault.

3. Victim stage: Allow yourself to feel you were a victim. This includes feeling helpless, hopeless, defeated, 'poor me,' discouraged, depressed, low energy, self-pity, and such. Engage the Welcoming Prayer with these feelings to work through them. Eventually you'll get tired of the victim stage and, after some reflection, it'll move into the victim-anger stage.

The first three steps in this forgiveness process (claiming your hurt, self-blame/guilt, and feeling a victim) take us down into places of sadness, loneliness, disappointment, emptiness, heartbreak, and heavy blues in the soul. The false self tries either to avoid these ego-deflating experiences or else wallows in them like a broken child. The final two or three stages (victim–anger, healthy anger, and acceptance/healing) bring us back up into places of active ego-strength, assertiveness, peace, and freedom in the soul. This is a resurgence of life-manifesting energy ranging from the vengeful ego-inflation and self-righteous delusions of victim–anger to the humble assertiveness of healthy anger, self-help and the inner peace of acceptance, compassion, and resolution that comes as the healing gift of forgiveness is completed deep inside us by the divine action.

4. Anger: This stage has two phases. First is victim–anger where you want to get back at whoever hurt you. You want to "get even." You want revenge. Allow yourself to feel it. You may feel rage and hatred toward the perpetrator and a desire to see her or him suffer as you've suffered. Feel it but do not act on it. Know that to harbor hatred and desire for revenge is to nourish an evil demon in the heart of one's soul. Self-restraint here is a dramatic purifying turning point in the process of forgiveness. Practicing the Welcoming Prayer with the ill will, hatred, and wrath of victim–anger serves to unload a train of toxic negativity from the Unconscious. Releasing this negativity serves to free the soul from the demonic grip of evil intentions and malicious desires.

Victim–anger comes from the root of false perspective in the soul's micro-spirituality spectrum and reinforces our false separate-self sense. Victim–anger is motivated by afflictive emotions such as fear, rage, hatred, and pride. It feeds negative energy into the false self's fear-based emotional happiness programs for security, esteem, and power. In many cases, anger and aggression are used by the ego as defenses against, and for denial of its underlying fears and feelings of insecurity. When we practice the Welcoming Prayer with any of these afflictive emotions, it serves to peel back the hidden layers of our emotional wounds. This reveals the truth of our soul and frees us from the blinding illusions created through our root of false perspective, which is grounded in fear and the false assumption of an absolute ego-identity. Working faithfully and patiently through the forgiveness process brings us to the root of true perspective in our soul, which is grounded in love and our true Self in Christ.

Destructive victim–anger focuses attention on the other person, the perpetrator of our wound. Victim–anger may be converted into healthy anger by changing our focus from the other person back onto our self, not simply as a victim but with outrage at the wrong that was done to us and a decision to take positive action: 1) to protect our self and never allow this to happen to us again. We may do this by watching for warning signs in other people's attitudes and behavior so we may avoid getting what we don't want from them, and 2) practice the inner work of self-inquiry and self-observation to eliminate unhealthy habits and start doing positive things for our self to make our life better. This is the healthy, positive way to redirect the negativity of victim–anger, which is destructive to self and others. In practicing the Welcoming Prayer with victim–anger (which focuses attention back to oneself), one might add to the letting-go litany: "I let go of my desire for revenge."

5. Acceptance/Healing: Continue repeating these steps and recalling what happened to you until you no longer feel ongoing pain from the hurt, no self-blame or guilt about what happened to you. You're not a victim NOW (you were a victim in the past). Accepting the truth of what happened and letting it go, you're not angry about it now but reconciled to the facts and at peace with what has happened.

This does not mean that you agree with it as being right or deserved. You're simply accepting it as a fact of your personal history, which you cannot change. Separating yourself from it in real time, you're able to view it objectively as a learning experience. Now you're free to put it behind you in the past, where it belongs. This healing of accepting reality allows you to become free from your past hurt's negative influences in the present and future.

You may use the creative visualization of a "bubble meditation" to work the five steps and facilitate this forgiveness process. Use a quiet space where you will not be disturbed. Begin with a brief prayer and a few slow deep breaths, relaxing into the present moment. If you have more time, start out with Centering Prayer and then proceed: With eyes closed, imagine yourself in a transparent bubble with Jesus (the master of forgiveness) there to help you. Have the person you need to forgive come to you in a separate transparent bubble that touches yours. You talk to that person, looking into her or his eyes and reviewing verbally to the other person everything that happened and how you felt; as much as you can remember. You tell the person you want to forgive them and then go as far as you can through the five above steps of the forgiveness process. At the end of this forgiveness meditation, you say that you forgive them for whatever hurt they caused you, whether intentionally or unintentionally; and ask them to do the same for you. Then you visualize the other person's bubble moving away from yours into space until it disappears.

Repeat this daily until you can go through all five of the forgiveness-process steps without feeling any negative energy when you visualize and recall in detail what was done to hurt you and how you felt in the various stages. This will take some time and a lot of daily repetition. Gradually, you'll notice a shift in the energy of your feelings as you review what happened to you. It may help to ponder the suffering and death of Jesus on the Cross and how, as he was dying, he asked the Father to "*forgive them; for they do not know what they are doing*" (Luke 23:34). On the deepest level, the same is true whenever one person does harm to another; that is, whatever we do unto one another we unknowingly do unto Christ and our deepest Self in one another.

At some point in our bubble meditation, we may ask the other person why they said or did whatever it was that hurt us? From this we may intuit that he or she was acting ignorantly, unconsciously, and/or out of her or his own unhealed pain. With this, we may begin to feel compassion for the person who hurt us—as Jesus did for those who unjustly condemned, tortured, and killed him. When we can recall our hurt and work through all five steps of this forgiveness process feeling acceptance, peace, and compassion for the perpetrator, then the painful event we needed to forgive is truly in the past and our healing is complete.

We cannot begin this Five-Step Forgiveness Process until we're ready to. In cases where a person is too hurt and angry to want to forgive, he or she may begin by praying for the perpetrator or for the grace to pray for and forgive the other person or persons. We cannot truly begin to forgive until a certain amount of healing takes place in our soul in relation to the hurt we've suffered and whom or what we need to forgive. Healing begins when we start to do something positive for our self (like practicing this forgiveness process), rather than passively remaining stuck in any of the five stages. Bringing unconscious contents up into consciousness automatically changes them. This begins with step one, claiming our hurt, and continues throughout all the steps of the process.

Forgiving someone does not mean we have to spend time with them, especially if it's a toxic individual who is liable to do us further harm. An essential aspect of healthy anger in step four is protecting our self from further injury, harm, and abuse by avoiding people, situations, and things that are not good for us. In such cases, where there's been a strong connection to an abusive person whom we need to forgive, in our bubble meditation we may visualize a ribbon shaped like an infinity sign tying our bubble and the other person's together. This ribbon symbolizes the bond between us and the other person. Each day, at the end of the visualization, imagine a large divine scissors cutting this connecting ribbon so that the two bubbles separate, with the other person's bubble floating away into empty space. As images move energy, this helps to sever unhealthy relationships. On the spiritual level, forgiving another person releases her or him and severs the knot of negative connection between two souls.

On the other hand, in cases where it's safe and both parties are willing, the forgiveness process may be further completed on the human level via physical communication and personal reconciliation among individuals who've experienced various forms of injury, hurt, betrayal, abuse, and misunderstanding. This may serve to bring people who genuinely love each other closer together than they were before; *if* they can learn from their mistakes, and grow in mutual understanding and compassion through honest self-disclosure and caring trust on the basis of a fresh start in their relationship. When people are unable to trust one another due to unhealed wounds of loss, abandonment, betrayal, rejection, and so on, this reconciliation and renewal of a budding or broken relationship may not be realistically possible. We need to be honest and realistic.

There's always some element of uncertainty in any human relationship, since people have free will and liberty to change their minds. This element of uncertainty serves to make the drama and game of God's Great Adventure more interesting. In the case of each human relationship, we need to intuit whom to trust and how much. Though there is uncertainty, there are also the odds or probabilities as to whether or not a particular individual may be reliable and worthy of our trust. Hence, each person needs to be her or his own psychologist in determining whom to trust, how much to trust, and whom not to trust. If God had wanted us to be one-way robots, we would not have been given free will.

VII

The forgiveness process cannot move forward as long as we hold onto grudges in the victim and victim–anger stages. Hating a perpetrator is often equated with loving her or his victim (our self or another) and honoring that person's memory. This self-righteous hate perpetuates refusal to forgive and feeds desires for cruel revenge in the victim–anger stage. It is what makes reconciliation so difficult in ongoing group conflicts of hatred, prejudice, and revenge-seeking (e.g., the Israelis and Palestinians). In such tragic situations, forgiving the enemy is identified with betraying the victims whom one loves so that, perversely, hating and harming the enemy is seen as an expression of our love for the enemy's victims with whom we identify. This is a deadly trap of Evil and the false self.

People are often seduced by the victim–anger stage and remain stuck there because the energy of anger makes them feel powerful, lifting them out of the wimpy helplessness of the gloomy victim stage with its apathy and depression. Victim–anger is an effective way of escaping from the first three stages of hurt, guilt, and victim in which the ego feels sad, weak, depressed, and deflated. The aggressive energy of victim–anger inflates the ego with delusional feelings of strength, aliveness, and self-righteousness. Unfortunately, victim–anger only perpetuates cycles of hatred and abuse and is actually cowardly because, underneath, it fears facing the truth of one's repressed feelings of hurt, guilt, and victim-stage afflictive emotions. The hatred and violent aggression of victim–anger are actually ego-defensive cover-ups for underlying feelings of fear, pain, and anxiety that have not been dealt with.

Minimizing, denying, or wallowing in our hurt keeps us stuck in the first step of the forgiveness process. The same is true for guilt (step two) and the victim stage (step three). It's necessary to go through and fully experience all the conscious and unconscious energy of each step in order to complete and release it. This is why we need to go back and keep working our way through the five steps. As long as any energy of a particular step remains in the Unconscious, the person stays stuck in that step and hasn't completed it. As we consent, cooperate, and are willing, the divine action heals our wounds in the Unconscious. Allowing unconscious contents to come up into consciousness and accepting them as our own automatically changes them and releases their energy. This is a basic virtue of the unloading process.

As we fully taste and digest the reality of our hurt, guilt, wounding, and wrath in working the five steps, we are challenged by God's inner presence and our true Self to transcend these very real insults. We do this by placing them in the past as we become positively proactive in learning from our experience, practicing self-protection, and taking constructive steps to make our life better. We do this in partnership with Christ, the divine healer within. As we begin experiencing the wellbeing and freedom of God's healing work in our soul, how we relate to our wounding and its consequences changes for the better. As we place the wrong that we've suffered and its perpetrator in the past, we begin to see them from an objective distance and in a new light.

We're no longer struggling or drowning in the thick toxic soup of our hurt, guilt, wounding, and anger. This new perspective allows us to feel a humble caring compassion for our self, other victims, and eventually the perpetrators—who we now see are also victims acting out of their own unhealed pain and anger. We realize that the only way humanity's tragic cycles of hatred, wounding, and abuse may be ended is through the process of forgiveness. This heartfelt insight frees us from the demon of our conscious and unconscious hatred, rage and pain, moving us up into the higher vantage point of a new perspective in relation to our own suffering and that of others. This is a healing conversion experience given by the Will of Divine Love awakening in our soul.

Forgiving others who have hurt us deeply is not easy; but, with God's help, it is definitely possible. Such forgiveness is a work of healing done in our soul by the Holy Spirit. As *love determines justice* and *will determines destiny*, the forgiveness process requires our willing consent and participation. It's a partnership with Christ in us that requires us doing our part. It cannot be done against our will. Hence, we need to grow into the will to forgive, which can only happen when we're ready to forgive.

Though forgiving others is not easy, self-forgiveness is more difficult still. Years ago, I learned that I cannot really respect, love, or esteem myself unless I honestly feel I'm worthy of my own respect and love. Whatever our egocentric standards may be, living in harmony with true conscience is the essential key to healthy self-esteem, respect, and love. Having unrealistic self-images and expectations based on unhealthy cultural conditioning and the false self's emotional happiness programs are primary obstacles to healthy self-esteem and authentic self-forgiveness, which need to be grounded in a realistic acceptance of our human limitations as well as a humble appreciation of our immense value as precious spiritual beings who are loved infinitely by God.

The need for self-forgiveness arises when we get stuck in self-blame and guilt, the second step in the Five-Step Forgiveness Process. We all make mistakes because we are all flawed and imperfect human beings. Accepting this fact, honestly recognizing our mistakes, which we sincerely regret, and moving forward in our life with the resolve to not continue repeating those mistakes, is a reasonable basis for healthy self-forgiveness. It's all that God asks of us to receive God's forgiveness; that is, admitting the truth, taking responsibility for our choices, actions, and their consequences, feeling sincerely sorry, and working to avoid repeating the same errors. If this is enough for God to forgive us, why isn't it enough for me to forgive myself? Do I know better than God in this matter of forgiveness? Of course not!

As William Blake writes in *The Marriage of Heaven and Hell*, "Shame is Pride's cloak."[11] This important psychological insight points to the fact that we often fail at self-forgiveness due to unrealistic self-images and expectations (ego-requirements) grounded in obsessive scruples, perfectionism, and false-self programming. A significant part of what makes self-forgiveness so difficult is what Sigmund Freud called the *tyrannical super-ego*. This is a false inner voice of conscience, lodged in the Unconscious, by which we judge our self harshly and unreasonably. It's composed of the negative repressive values we've internalized from parents and society. As we identify with and internalize our cultural conditioning, we unconsciously become its obedient slave, for better or worse. Only the authentic spiritual values of the Will of Divine Love may free us from unhealthy cultural conditioning and the anti-values of Evil and the false-self system that make self-forgiveness so difficult.

To practice self-forgiveness, we may do a "double-bubble" meditation with our self where we engage an ongoing dialogue between the part of our self that needs to forgive and the part of our self that needs to be forgiven. In Jungian terms, this may be seen as a dialogue between our *persona* (conscious personality) and our *shadow* (the rejected, wounded parts of our soul). It's like having a self-conversation while looking in a mirror. We visualize the "guilty" part of our self in its own bubble facing the "accusing" part in its own bubble. We alternate identifying with these two parts of our self and playing their roles inside us. The "accusing" part tells the "guilty" part what we need to forgive it for and why. Then, identifying with the "guilty" part of our self, we respond by telling the "accusing" part, as best we can, what we did and why we did it. Then, expressing our regret, we ask for forgiveness. This self-forgiveness process involves going back and forth between these two parts of our soul in dialogue.

In the course of this inner dialogue, we may learn that the "accusing" part of our self also needs forgiveness for how it's denied, rejected, and treated the "guilty" part. This self-forgiveness dialogue is to continue daily—with each side expressing its feelings and asking for forgiveness—until a mutually compassionate reconciliation is reached and the two parts of our divided self may join together in a single bubble. That is, we continue working at self-forgiveness until the two opposed parts of our self merge their separate bubbles and intra-self identities together into one unified self. Then this healing, which integrates the shadow-self into the conscious-self, will be complete and the energy of the soul's inner conflict will be released for positive, life-giving uses. Honesty, compassionate self-acceptance and letting go of unrealistic expectations, demands, and false self-images are essential for working through this self-forgiveness process, which may, over time, involve a detailed life review and is done in the presence and with the help of our true conscience, Higher Self or Christ in us.

There's a legitimacy and value to *everything* we feel, even our afflictive emotions. The healing process of forgiveness is not a question of getting rid of our hurt, self-blame, victim blues, and victim-anger—unpleasant and painful as these may be. It's actually a question of honestly facing, feeling, accepting, honoring, and embracing these natural human emotions in order not to mindlessly act them out but to go through and integrate them into the wholeness of our conscious identity. This process changes them from foes into allies. To deny or reject an emotion is to deny, reject, and invalidate the part of our self that feels it. This is dishonest and divides us from our self. It weakens us and compromises our integrity.

When we honestly feel, accept, and integrate our emotions—especially the afflictive ones—they become a source of strength and wisdom in us. This is what the healing process is all about—to become free to feel *all* of our legitimate emotions, without being overwhelmed or taken over by them. It's been said that scar tissue from a healed wound is stronger than unscarred tissue that's never been wounded. This is true in the soul as well as in the physical body.

Of course, we need the healthy ego-strength, self-control, and freedom to consciously decide what to do or not do with our powerful emotions when we experience them. Two common reasons people deny or repress powerful emotions are: 1) They are too overwhelming and destabilizing for the conscious ego; and 2) we fear they may lead us to do something we will regret if we give in to them and act them out. In other words, there's a deep fear of losing control. These are legitimate reasons for restraining or repressing emotions we're not ready to face, at least up to a point and especially in early life. Lacking sufficient ego-strength, a person may get swallowed up into an afflictive emotion so that it takes over and becomes her or his center of identity. When this is a temporary experience, it may lead to deep personal insight and healing. If it's a permanent or randomly recurring experience, however, and if the person feels compelled to act out an afflictive emotion, it may become quite dangerous. Hence, we need to engage intense afflictive emotions and our dark side in a supportive therapeutic setting, with a trusted friend, or in the context of prayer under the protection of spiritual guidance.

At some point, we'll need to face our repressed emotional issues and work through them, if we're to experience healing, become fully whole and integrated. Emotions do not lie. They are part of the truth of our soul and reveal us to our self; if we can pay attention and go deeply into them with patience, tolerance, and humility and under the protection of our spiritual center. Emotions span the spectrum of our soul's micro-spirituality and are to be welcomed, owned, and integrated. Through engaging the forgiveness process, we may work through our afflictive emotions into love as the healing of forgiveness opens the soul to humble tears of compassion and compunction, caring and self-giving wherein our giving becomes receiving the goodness of God's Love.

VIII

Since prehistoric times, dreams have occupied a central place in the inner life of humanity. Freud called dreams *"the royal road to the Unconscious."* There are several kinds of dreams and a variety of theories attempting to explain their origins and significance, or lack thereof. Each of these theories sheds light but tends to focus on a particular type of dream to the exclusion of others. For example, dreams may be regarded strictly as intra-psychic events created by the Unconscious within the soul, as in the modern theories of Sigmund Freud and Carl Jung, who viewed dreams differently in terms of their respective theories. This approach has revealed a lot of value for both theory and practice regarding the soul's inner life in the context of our modern world.

Much older traditions and mythologies, dating back to prehistory, refer to dreams as out-of-body wanderings of the soul during sleep in various regions of the spirit world and throughout creation's metaphysical heavens and underworld. The shamanic practices of humanity's oldest religions bear witness to this, as do ancient pagan traditions of magic, occultism, witchcraft, and Nature worship, which could be used for harming or healing people. There are clairvoyant dreams and visions that foreshadow future events in the physical world; and retrospective dreams that take us into the past. There are telepathic dreams involving communication with non-physical spiritual guides and teachers who may instruct and inspire us; and dreams involving communication with less evolved spirits and souls. The Bible has many examples of dreams and visions, which people often looked to for guidance, insight, and warnings (e.g., Pharaoh's dreams regarding the years of plague in ancient Egypt interpreted by Joseph, the imprisoned son of Jacob, and Pilate's wife's dream regarding Jesus).

Several possibilities exist regarding what dreams may be. Some schools of mystical theology (e.g., Hinduism), and philosophical idealism (e.g., Bishop George Berkeley), regard God's Great

Adventure and all of created reality as the Great Cosmic Dream of passing time and duality happening within the eternal Divine Consciousness of non-created Reality. In other words, the human experience is sometimes regarded as a particular kind of individual and collective dream we are all experiencing together—with God dreaming us and we dreaming each other and God, or at least our ideas of God. Such views may offer valuable insights into the relativity and mystery of our existence in created reality; but they may also be used to deny its rich spiritual meaning, value, and potential in favor of some life-negating, other-worldly orientation (e.g., the heresy of Manicheanism).

I suspect that people today generally do not value or pay as much attention to dreams as in times past; since we now have easy access to an overwhelming stream of images, news, advertising, and entertainment via the mass marketing of various electronic media—radio, movies, television, videos, the internet, and so on. Yet still we dream. The question is this: Do we remember or relate to our dreams in a meaningful way? The answer will vary from one person to another. Dreams are direct communication from the Unconscious. If we dismiss or ignore them as generally insignificant, then we shall remember them less and our relationship to the Unconscious through dreams will not be able to develop into a meaningful exchange of communication. As we relate to the Unconscious, it responds back to us in return. Hence, if we take an interest in our dreams as meaningful, and make some effort to honor, recall, or record them, then we'll tend to experience and remember more and more details of them.

Intra-psychic dreams reveal things that are happening in the Unconscious within the soul. How the Unconscious relates to the conscious mind through dreams depends significantly on our personal history, and on the contents of the conscious mind—that is, on our particular worldview and what's currently going on in our personal experience of the drama and game of God's Great Adventure. For example, when I was studying or thinking about Freudian Psychoanalysis, I had dreams with symbolism relating to these ideas. When reading or thinking in terms of Jungian Psychology, I tend to have dreams reflecting Jung's theory of the Unconscious. My point here is that the Unconscious cooperates by addressing us in terms of *whatever* conceptual language or symbolism we're consciously relating to or conversant in, either currently or historically. The Unconscious may address us through dreams in terms of erotic symbolism, religious symbolism, social, cultural, political, or personally historical symbolism; whatever is on or in our mind.

Dreams may be relatively obscure, simple, and straightforward, or, as we engage and relate to them as meaningful and important, they may become quite complex, multilayered, revelatory, or puzzling. They are always unique and specific to the individual who dreams them. Like riddles written in profound symbolic code, dreams are often subtle or shocking allegories expressing what is going on within our physical body and soul. The Unconscious is incredibly creative and, like God, often full of surprises, humor, and unexpected juxtapositions of contraries and opposites.

We may work with our Unconscious by working consciously with our dreams. As Carl Jung points out, many dreams are compensatory as the Transcendent Function (divine action) in the Unconscious creates dream contents designed to counteract conscious attitudes and actions that are out of harmony and balance with objective reality. The humiliating self-knowledge experienced in Centering Prayer via the unloading process, which reveals to us the hidden truth of our soul, is an important example of the Unconscious compensating for and correcting imbalances and illusions in our conscious mind and outlook. Dreams may play a significant role in the process of unloading the Unconscious, thus contributing to the soul's inner purification and healing.

If we relate to the Unconscious as a teacher and ally, it can be of valuable help to us through dreams and in other ways. This, of course, requires an attitude of trust toward the Unconscious, which makes sense when our sincere intentions and goals are in alignment with those of our true spiritual Self, the central governing archetype or divine indwelling in the human Unconscious. If, like Carl Jung, we approach the Unconscious with an attitude of humility, respect, and even reverence, it will respond to us in helpful and instructive ways. Our relationship to dreams and the Unconscious is really not separate from our personal relationship to our deep inner Self and God.

The Unconscious responds to everything we think, feel, say, and do. To work with the Unconscious through dreams, we may begin by asking it, before going to sleep, to give us a dream, and to help us remember our dream. Then we may start keeping a dream diary, recording in words and pictures whatever we remember from our dreams. This may, at times, require getting up in the night to record our dream contents as soon as possible. Experience teaches that if we wait until later, we will not be able to remember all details of our dream or maybe even the dream itself. With practice, this becomes habitual and easier, and launches us on an interesting new adventure into the depths of our soul. Go back and review your dream diary, looking for patterns and themes in your dreams. It's very important for each person to learn and develop her or his own unique personal dream-symbolism, as revealed by the Unconscious. As with Centering Prayer, we gradually learn to interpret and work with our dreams by taking time and continuing to just do it.

IX

The Unconscious plays a key role in the drama and game of God's Great Adventure. All manner of communications, from within and from without the individual soul, may be felt, seen and heard through our dreams and other expressions of the Unconscious. These expressions may range from the intra-psychic unloading of the Unconscious and workings of the Divine Therapy, to a variety of communications coming from outside the individual soul. Intuitions of creativity, desire, and divine inspiration may all come to us through the Unconscious. The imagination is a primary instrument through which the Unconscious communicates; and some of the dreams it produces are known to be intuitive sources of creativity and insight in both science and the arts.

As human beings created in the divine image and likeness, we are all born with a basic instinctual need to express ourselves through creative activity, in order to externalize and give voice to what is within us, and to communicate with others around us. This is necessary for our health, wellbeing, and growth, and in human relationships. We discover and become ourselves through creative self-expression. There are innumerable ways in which we may do this (e.g., through movement, thought, speech, action, appearance, work, play, and the arts). There is an art to *everything*, when we do it consciously as creative self-expression in the present moment; especially when we put our heart and soul into it.

With the right motivation and receptivity, art may be a path to spiritual growth and inner transformation for those who deeply experience it, as well as for those who create it. It's all about the communication of meanings, values, life experience, and the transmission of micro-spiritual energy and consciousness from one soul to another or others. In the most outstanding and extraordinary cases, art may involve a transmission of Macro-Spiritual Energy and Consciousness from one soul to another, or possibly many others. This may be through drama, music, literature, poetry, dance, the visual arts, or any form of creative self-expression involving energy exchanges of authentic self-disclosure, passion, intimacy, or love communicated from one soul to another.

It is liberating for us to honestly, freely, and effectively express our self, as this releases energies from within us. When we allow our self to be spontaneous and not constrained by fears of the ego, unconscious contents may be released into consciousness and we may learn something new about our self and how we feel. We need a safe context, such as an intimate relationship with our self, God, or another person, in which to do this. The creative arts also offer a safe context where, within the structured bounds of our chosen genre (e.g., acting, music, writing), we may let our self go and freely express *whatever* comes out of us. This is the beginning of the creative process wherein what we come up with is a raw, uncensored expression of our inner state of being. The uninhibited play and creativity of such honest self-expression becomes a liberating act of self-discovery, releasing something that was pent-up within us. It may reveal the unconscious contents of any places in the soul's micro-spiritual spectrum; and this release of energy may be enjoyable, exhilarating or disturbing.

Bringing something that was unconscious and held inside us up into consciousness via creative self-expression releases and changes its energy, directly affecting our state of being. As with any unloading of the Unconscious, the crucial question is: *What* shall we choose to do with these newly released unconscious contents? This makes all the difference. Do we simply express our raw inspirations as they are, giving in to them and impulsively acting them out? Or do we exercise restraint, so we may work upon and refine them into something more evolved?

Creative self-expression and the arts as spiritual path often involve the labor and process of cultivating and integrating the original raw material we began with into something finer and more evolved. The raw material that comes out of us may be crude and immature, expressing our own unrefined, wounded state of being, which we may be reluctant to disclose to our self or others. Conflict generates creativity, and some artists require it to do their art. Such individuals are often tortured souls, divided and tormented within by the pain of unhealed wounds and unresolved issues. The creation and perfection of their art is a practical means through which artists may externalize what's within them and work to redeem themselves by resolving these inner conflicts. In such cases, doing art as an end in itself requires commitment and courage to face our demons, and it becomes true therapy for the soul's inner healing and growth. Integrity in the soul is born of honesty and originality in self-expression.

An artist's inner motivation functions as an essential key to the spiritual outcome of her or his creative endeavors. This motivation may come from the false self or the true Self, or from both as mixed motivation. When self-expression is inspired by higher, more evolved energies from the Unconscious, then the artist's challenge is to work through and overcome the resistance and obstacles posed by her or his false-self system, dark side, and wounded state of being; in order to faithfully express and communicate the higher inspiration without distorting or degrading it. The struggle to do this involves humbly asking for inner help and guidance, confronting one's obstacles, exercising patient persistence, and faithfully following the lead of what the Unconscious (divine action) suggests. This struggle and its process reveal the truth of the artist's soul and contribute directly to her or his spiritual growth.

We may well ask: How does the creative process of artwork act as a spiritual path? The creative process begins in consciousness, often unexpectedly, with an idea triggered by some life experience. It may be inspiration from above and/or the spontaneous, uncensored release of unconscious contents from below that show the inner truth of an artist's soul. This supplies the raw material for the creative process. The artist is one with her or his work, which is also creative play. The raw material is an expression of the artist's being and he or she is intimately identified with it. As the raw material of original idea is worked upon, cultivated, and refined, the spiritual alchemy of the creative process transmutes its energy *and* the being of the artist simultaneously. This gradually transmutes the artist into a "new creation." Since the artist is one with her or his work, as it evolves and transforms, so does the artist. This is the basic principle of art as a spiritual path. It applies to all forms and genres of artistic self-expression. However, its practical effectiveness depends upon the purity and sincerity of the artist's motivation; that is, whether it's of the false self or the true Self. Doing art for our true whole Self is living prayer and worship.

Creative energy, whether sexual, emotional, mental, psychic, social, spiritual, or artistic, is sacred energy and needs to be respected as such. It is union energy, ultimately leading to the conscious union of the individual soul with the Divine Love of non-created-Reality. The mystery of creativity involves the sublimation of our instinctual life-force energy into art, science, culture, and civilization. Consciousness is the crown of sexuality, the highest expression of our life-force energy. Art as a spiritual path consciously expresses and reveals the truth of the human condition and soul. It is ultimately religious, not in the sense of formal organized religion but in the sense of freely expressing and revealing the soul naked in the awesome mystery of its life-giving Source. The spiritual mission of art is to reveal the full truth of the soul (its dark and light sides), express the beauty and goodness of God's creation, and, with the help of divine inspiration, bring the soul home to its holy center in the love, truth, and freedom of non-created Reality. This is also the mission of true religion—to take us consciously back to our sacred Origins.

X

The immortal genius of divine creativity gives rise to endless variety and uniqueness in expressing the universal archetypes of what may be in the drama and game of God's Great Adventure. As humans are created in the divine image and likeness, this principle of divine originality is clearly reflected in the unique personal symbolism of each individual soul's Unconscious, where creation's universal themes and archetypes are expressed in relatively and sometimes utterly novel ways, such as in dreams. Each moment of time and each individual soul are unique and may never be exactly duplicated because, in created reality, everything is in motion and always changing. Consequently, no abstract psychological theory, theology, or philosophy may ever possibly account for all the diverse variety and uniqueness happening in God's creation, in human souls, and in real life as it's lived and experienced by real people.

Scientific theories, theology, and philosophical models of God's creation and the human soul may classify their subject matter into general, abstract categories; but they cannot account for the endless creative diversity and uniqueness experienced by individual souls and human consciousness in the concrete reality of actual life. This important fact points to the intellectual error and life-negating danger of limiting our appreciation and understanding of the mysteries of God's creation and human souls to any kind of philosophical, theological, or psychological reductionism—in which human consciousness and real life experiences are reduced to the limited, lifeless categories of abstract theories, models, and terminology. To succumb to the fallacy of reductionism is to mistake a map for the actual territory it represents.

Maps may be very helpful as guides to practice; but only to the degree that they are accurate and actually cover the territory we wish to explore. Theoretical maps may never serve as adequate substitutes for actually exploring the territory they're designed to represent. To reduce unconscious contents or real lived experiences to abstract concepts and categories; as, for example, if we intellectualize our emotions to avoid actually feeling them; is a tragic violation of life's dynamic creative reality and the soul's integrity.[12] We are so much more than that, and the gift of our life is an ever-astonishing miracle.

Some of the best psychologists are playwrights and novelists who take audiences inside the soul and consciousness of their fictional characters. These discreet examples present the inner workings of individual human personalities in the drama and game of God's Great Adventure as no general "one-size-fits-all" theories may possibly do. In this sense, fictional individual case examples portrayed by creative artists are far truer to real life as it's lived and experienced than are conceptual categories of abstract theories. Art reflects life and reality, expressing their beauty, ugliness, and complex spiritual dimensions as people experience them. Well-executed art is a door to our own inner depths and healing as the soul's micro- and Macro-Spiritual dimensions may be experienced in great and not-so-great art. It is we who decide which is which. The best and brightest is that which awakens love in us. For different people, this will obviously be found in different works and styles of art.

Our individual stories are clearly a primary source of personal identity and uniqueness in the human condition and game of God's Great Adventure. While this is certainly true on the human level, there's also a radical sense in which all our stories are lies, fictions of the dream that lends absolute reality to the false separate-self sense and its emotional programs for happiness. This seemingly revolutionary perspective that sees all our personal stories as lies (because they are stories about the false self or ego, which is itself a lie) was taught by Paul Ilecki (1950–2014), who created the contemplative "Just Noticing" psycho-spiritual practice.[13] Paul Ilecki was truly an ambassador of love, much appreciated and well beloved by those who knew him here in Alaska, where I live, and elsewhere.

Just Noticing is a simple practice for living immediately and deeply in awareness of the present moment without being caught up in the ego-drama of our personal story. Rather than viewing life and reality through the eyes of our emotional happiness programs and false self, the Just Noticing practice invites us to put those distractions aside, if we can, and open to the depth dimension of the immediate present moment, which is spacious, peaceful, restful, nonconceptual, and rich in the wellbeing of God's silent presence and abiding love. Paul Ilecki was a fully human, living example of this gift.

Paul, who was also a teacher of the *Ira Progoff Intensive Journal Program*, referred to Just Noticing practice as "awareness noticing" and "a form of un-journaling" for contemplatives. Paul wrote,

> Awareness noticing relies on short written observations that are simply put aside in the act of turning to the next awareness that arises.... Awareness noticing relies on non-attachment to self and ego by opening to an enlarged field of awareness, oneness, non-separation and the wisdom inherent in all beings...It is simply a way of holding life's experiences and awareness in consciousness (and in writing) only long enough to give those events and awarenesses sufficient attention before letting them flow by, onto the next awareness or experience. The cumulative effect of this "journaling" documentation is the development of subtle habits that become patterns of awareness that are prolonged without attachment to ego, emotions, addictions or destructive behavior.[14]

What follows is my interpretation of Just Noticing. I'd hoped to review it with Paul before finalizing it; but, unfortunately, that's no longer possible. I discussed this with Paul and also how his Just Noticing practice reminded me of the Welcoming Prayer. They have some obvious similarities but are definitely two distinct practices in relation to the Unconscious. That is, Welcoming Prayer embraces and works through what comes up from the Unconscious (see pages 138–142); while Just Noticing openly acknowledges and releases whatever arises in consciousness in order to enter into and abide in the deeper nonconceptual Unconscious. In the context of Just Noticing, we notice that the naked present moment is colored, layered over, and filtered by our thoughts and particular perceptions—as in Centering Prayer, where "thoughts" are all perceptions in the stream of our consciousness. The aim in Just Noticing is to abide deeper, so that what's "above the river" of consciousness—that is, all particular perceptions may become integrated into what's "below the river" in an open field of awareness grounded in the present moment. This represents a radical change of perspective in living daily life, a shift of focus from false self to true self.

My own sense is that Welcoming Prayer is a good preliminary to prepare the soul for the Just Noticing practice—as I'll try to explain. In our discussions, Paul and I were not able to resolve fully the question of comparing Welcoming Prayer, which I'd practiced since 1992, to Just Noticing, which he certainly knew and understood far better than I did. In what follows, I'll express my views and try to be true to Paul's teaching of Just Noticing as I understand it. Like Centering Prayer or the Welcoming Prayer, Just Noticing may be learned only by doing it again and again.

To begin Just Noticing practice, sit down with a pen and small disposable notebook. Notice what stands out in your immediate awareness—a thought, feeling, body sensation, sight, sound, odor, memory, and so on—and write down what it is. If nothing stands out, recall some person, event, or experience of significance, and write down whatever you notice. After simply experiencing awareness of whatever you notice, write in a brief note, which may be one or a few words, and let this pass so you can notice whatever awareness you experience next. Continue doing this for a set period of time, which could be five minutes, ten minutes, or longer.

When doing this practice, notice any associations that may come up in response to each moment of awareness; but do not deliberately fantasize, spin a story, commentary or engage in any self-talk around what you notice. Simply write down what you notice and move on to the next awareness. If you notice you're engaging in self-talk, and the like, stop it; write that down and see what you notice, remaining non-attached to the specific contents of consciousness and openly present to the immediate moment. This describes the basic Just Noticing process, which is a subtle witnessing and responding practice of self-observation undertaken without focusing on an ego-self.

Continue doing this daily and notice what happens. You'll find a subtle shift in your patterns of awareness as you move from one moment of noticing to another. It becomes easier to freely experience and release your moments of awareness without commenting at length about them. You may begin to notice a quiet space opening up within these moments of awareness. This space resembles the space of nonconceptual silence and inner absorption you may sometimes experience in Centering Prayer. There is consciousness but no specific object or content. It's a state of restful abiding peace that is always present within or under the phenomena of passing experience. You can't notice this abiding space while you're in it because it's always there, has great depth but no opposite with which to compare it. It's a state of non-dual awareness we may notice *after* the fact.

In speaking of Just Noticing, Paul Ilecki used the metaphor of "the river of consciousness," with time and space, ordinary dualistic awareness, the human condition and the drama and game of God's Great Adventure *above* the river, and the spacious place of timeless abiding inner absorption and peace *below* the river in the Ground Unconscious. We notice the phenomena of passing experience arise out of and return into the Unconscious, which is the place of abiding in our true Self beyond yet within the passing show of created reality. This is the ubiquitous, ever-present place of the divine presence and action within where we are "taken" in receiving the gift of *apophatic* (nonconceptual) contemplation.

The Just Noticing practice peels back the filters of the present moment and is designed to help us "drop down" into the river's peaceful abiding depths in our true spiritual center, so we may balance and integrate our contemplative practice and this always-present inner awareness with our roles, activities, and consciousness in daily life. Humility, compassion, and the gospel values of love and forgiveness grow out of this ground of our inner being, which holds our true center and life in Christ. In contrast to and apart from the reality of this inner spiritual ground, our stories, games, and separate-self identity "above the river" are illusions and lies that ensnare and enslave us. Yet, from the deeper perspective of the abiding Divine Consciousness, these illusions and lies are all part of the truth of what is, if we can notice it. This divine presence within is thus the ultimate unconscious content intended by the Will of Divine Love to ultimately become Pure Consciousness in us.

XI

When writing down what is noticed, you may tear the pages out of your small notebook and throw them away. Or you may keep them to review and dispose of later. Writing down our noticed moments of awareness acknowledges them, and throwing away the pages and words symbolizes releasing or letting go of our passing experiences "above the river." This helps to cultivate a habit of non-attachment or non-possessiveness in relation to temporary things. Eventually, the habit of Just Noticing developed during daily formal practice may be integrated into daily life in relation to whatever catches our attention. By simply noticing and letting go of these particular conscious contents, we may remain grounded in the openness of the living present moment, rather than drifting into overlapping commentaries of unnecessary self-talk and ego-fantasy that separate us from the depth dimension of presence that's always here, "under the river" beneath surface appearances. In other words, Just Noticing may help us to remain more fully present in daily life and keep us from becoming lost into and over-identified with our role and involvement in the drama and game of God's Great Adventure.

However (and this is where I may differ from or not fully grasp Paul Ilecki's teaching), there are emotionally charged contents that come up into consciousness—such as episodes of intense or prolonged unloading—that we can't simply take conscious note of and then put aside to move on to whatever comes up next. The reason for this is that these contents can be quite overwhelming, as they rush forth from within us, persist, and temporarily take over our consciousness. We can't just notice and drop them because they need to be released, accepted, and are coming up from deep inside us, from under the river of consciousness.

My sense is that a person's liberty to practice Just Noticing under all circumstances will depend on how wounded or healed they are. The stronger a person's false self and its emotional happiness programs are, the more he or she will need the Divine Therapy and *kataphatic* practices, like the Welcoming Prayer and Five-Step Forgiveness Process, to get healed and liberated from the negative influence

HUMAN CONDITION

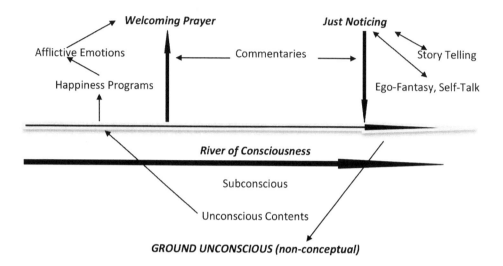

of toxic unconscious contents such as misguided desires and afflictive emotions. As the reservoir of pent-up power is gradually drained from the false-self system's energy centers, the frequency and intensity of afflictive emotions will reduce. As inner wounds heal, symptoms subside, and inner peace grows in the soul, Just Noticing practice, inner relaxation, and peaceful abiding in the immediate present will become easier, more natural, and increasingly effective.

Until such time, Just Noticing may be effectively used in relatively undisturbed moments for avoiding ego-distractions of idle fantasy, minor irritations, and habitual self-talk patterns that are not charged with strong, compelling emotional content from unconscious wounds and happiness programs. When we're facing unhealthy habits (personal demons) that are stronger than our will to resist them, we do not have the liberty to "just notice" them and move on unaffected into the present moment. Other measures are needed (the Way of the Cross, Welcoming Prayer, or Five-Step Forgiveness Process), because their hold on us is such that we're not yet free to simply let them go. In this context, Just Noticing is an advanced psycho-spiritual practice that is most fully, freely, and effectively undertaken in a relatively post-false-self soul; that is, a soul not overly dominated by the false-self system with its emotional happiness programs and afflictive emotions.

XII

Learning to effortlessly abide in the nonconceptual spaciousness of the present moment within the drama and game of God's Great Adventure is a spiritual gift or skill that comes from non-attachment to ego and relative freedom from false-self compulsions such as a need to be in control. In such cases, Just Noticing is a simple way of moving from what's happening "above the river" into a non-dual consciousness that's grounded "under the river," in the *apophatic* true Self of the soul's divine indwelling deep in the Unconscious. We call it "the Unconscious" because it is unconscious to us, in our limited and evolving individual souls and consciousness. An inner attitude of reverent receptive silence is perhaps our best self-expressive spiritual symbol or gesture for relating to the Unconscious, which holds the potential of all possibilities. The Unconscious *is* the unknown. It is mystery, the elusive answer to the riddle of our deepest longing in the drama and game of God's Great Adventure. In each of us, the creative powers of the Unconscious come forth from the central Source of divine wisdom, understanding, and beauty hidden deep in our soul's true center. The mystery of creativity, fanning out in all directions, is a mystery of the Spirit breathing new energy and life into the soul from within. All of this happens through the agency of the Unconscious.

In its deepest depth, the Unconscious is a universal presence with a non-created, non-dual Consciousness of its own. It is the Divine Presence of non-created Reality, and its Transcendent Function is the Will of Divine Love, the basic motive force underlying created reality and the Laws governing it. Hence, the ultimate unconscious content is the divine presence, which holds in its Self all that is or may be. The ultimate destination of each soul's spiritual journey through created reality is to fully awaken into this presence. As long as we're human, however, we shall continue to have an Unconscious and to live in relation to it. The better we know our Unconscious, the better we know ourselves. The creative energy and activities of the Unconscious are what dreams are made of, whether they are sleeping dreams or waking ones.

The seven psycho-spiritual practices outlined in this chapter: 1) using an active prayer sentence; 2) the inner work of self-inquiry and self-observation; 3) Welcoming Prayer; 4) the Five-Step Forgiveness Process; 5) dream work; 6) creative self-expression and the arts; and 7) Just Noticing, are all best done in the context of a daily Centering Prayer or other nonconceptual meditative practice. These are all ways of cooperating with the divine action to purify, heal, and transform our soul and consciousness. Which of these practices to work with, and when to use them, is up to the discretion of the individual reader as he or she follows the inner guidance and inspiration of the Holy Spirit. For further information about these practices, please refer to the chapter notes and references regarding them. For Christians, all of these practices may engage the Way of The Cross.

The normal human condition is a state of being stuck or trapped "above the river," where we perceive the drama and game of God's Great Adventure we're in to be all that there is. The contemplative spiritual journey and Will of Divine Love aim to free us from this limiting illusion by giving us direct firsthand access to our soul's multifaceted inner life and the deeper transcendent truth of spiritual wealth that's always present in us, "under the river" in the heart of our Source.

8

FURTHER REACHES OF
EVOLVING CONSCIOUSNESS

FROM INDIVIDUAL TO UNIVERSAL CONSCIOUSNESS
ON THE TREE OF LIFE

The Qabalistic Tree of Life is a Master Symbol and comprehensive map of evolving consciousness, the individual soul, and Universal Creation (see chapter 1). It is made up of ten Holy Spheres divided into Three Triads plus the Kingdom Sphere of the individual human body and vast Physical Universe at the bottom. There is a smaller Tree of Life contained within each of the ten Spheres on the Tree. Each Sphere represents a general level of evolving consciousness in the soul's journey of return from the Kingdom Sphere of physical incarnation back up the Tree to its Source in the Crown Sphere and Limitless Light of non-created Reality.

Human ground in the drama and game of God's Great Adventure, where Good and Evil vie for dominion, and individual souls struggle for freedom, happiness, and fulfillment of their destinies as spiritual beings, consists of the physical Kingdom Sphere at the bottom of the Tree and the Personality/Astral Triad just above it. This is the realm of human free will wherein we create our personal angels and demons, and where we engage the limitations, conflicts, and creativity of the human condition. The soul evolves through these four Spheres by learning their spiritual lessons and climbing the individual Trees of Life within them. These are all Spheres of individual, separate-self consciousness, and their respective lessons challenge us to learn of Good and Evil as we grow in practical wisdom and integrity of character via a variety of experiences, relationships, and the practice of morality, ethics, and spiritual virtue in relating to others, our self, God, and God's creation. Growth in love is the essential key to our spiritual growth and consciousness evolution.

At some point we evolve from the consciousness and limitations of the Personality/Astral Triad up into the Spiritual/Moral Triad above it. The alchemical Sphere of Christ/Beauty on the Middle Pillar is the bottom Sphere of the Spiritual/Moral Triad and Central Sphere on the Tree of Life. This is the Sphere of the soul's divine indwelling and the Spiritual/Moral Triad is the Triad of the soul's individual spiritual ground. Individual consciousness is perfected in the Spiritual/Moral Triad.

The Christ/Beauty Sphere integrates all the energies of the soul in all its Spheres, and is the center of the divine action or Transcendent Function that unites the opposites to harmonize, balance, and align the false or lower self in the Personality/Astral Triad with the true or Higher Self above it in the Spiritual/Moral Triad. Manifesting the Will of Divine Love, Christ/Beauty also integrates the higher energies from the divine Spheres above it with the evolving energies of the personality Spheres below it. The Severity Sphere of the Spiritual/Moral Triad brings the soul's individual will into complete harmony and alignment with holy righteousness and the Laws of Cosmic Justice. The Spiritual/Moral Triad's Mercy Sphere establishes the individual soul in the non-dual principle and foundation of universal love and compassion for all. This is the Sphere of the Masters of Compassion, which marks the culmination and perfection of the soul as an individual consciousness in the service of the Will of Divine Love at the top of the Spiritual/Moral Triad.

All souls in the Spiritual/Moral Triad, having aligned their wills with the Will of Divine Love, actively function in various ways as spiritual guides and teachers in service to the divine plan unfolding in evolving souls in the Spheres below them. At the same time, these highly evolved individual souls, who are sometimes referred to as initiates, adepts, and masters, work on their own continuing spiritual growth and consciousness evolution as living, conscious conduits for the even higher energies that flow into the Spiritual/Moral Triad from the Supernal Triad above it, in the upper region of the Macrocosmic

Tree of Life. The Supernal Triad is the Triad of the soul's universal spiritual ground manifesting a variety of universal energies and consciousnesses. It represents an order of existence in nearness to God (non-created Reality) that we may scarce imagine.

Climbing the smaller Tree of Life in the Mercy Sphere of the Spiritual/Moral Triad marks a completion phase in the development of an individual soul and consciousness. At some point, the Master of Compassion will make the Great Journey across the Abyss separating the Spiritual/Moral and Supernal Triads. This Abyss corresponds to the invisible, nonconceptual Sphere on the Tree of Life known as "Daath/the Cloud." It is the unknowable Sphere of passage through the dark nights of the soul traversed in the smaller Tree within all the Spheres of the Tree. This dark, unconscious Sphere holds the evolving gift of *apophatic* contemplation into which Centering Prayer leads us.[1]

The Great Journey from the Mercy Sphere at the Top of the Spiritual/Moral Triad into the Sphere of Understanding at the bottom of the Supernal Triad is said to require a lengthy period of preparation. It's said to also require great inner strength because it involves the death of the soul's separate individual consciousness and its rebirth into a nascent Universal Consciousness in the Womb of God as Divine Mother in the Holy Sphere of Understanding. This is the Divine Womb in which all individual souls are formed and born into life and existence in created reality (see pages 8–9).[2] The individual soul's conscious return to this Womb of God is a great homecoming that initiates a radically new and greater phase in its evolving consciousness and life.

A Universal Consciousness co-participates in some degree in the non-dual Divine Consciousness that permeates the entire Tree of Life and all of created reality. What this is remains utterly inconceivable to any individual consciousness below the Spiritual/Moral Triad on the Tree of Life and, no doubt, may be only vaguely or partially conceivable to those higher evolved individual souls abiding relatively permanently in the Spheres of the Spiritual/Moral Triad. Glimpses of the heavenly Spheres of the Spiritual/Moral and Supernal Triads may, at times, be granted by divine grace and mercy through the agencies of Christ (the divine indwelling) and non-physical spiritual guides in the Higher Spheres of the Tree. Julian of Norwich's *Revelations of Divine Love*, Meister Eckhart's profound theological writings, the works of Christian Mystics like Teresa of Avila and John of the Cross, and Paul's contemplative spiritual visions as recorded in his New Testament letters, may all be examples of enlightening words and ideas inspired by such higher states of consciousness which—in terms of the Qabalistic Tree of Life—involve direct intuitive experiences of Spheres in the Spiritual/Moral and Supernal Triads, such as Julian's vision of all creation as a fragile "hazelnut" in God's hand.

From the formative Womb of Divine Mother in the Supernal Triad, the Master Soul eventually evolves into the Universal-Consciousness Wisdom Sphere of Divine Father or God, the Father, which corresponds to "the workings of the Universe." Here further access and participation are gained to all that is happening throughout created reality in all the Spheres of the Macrocosmic Tree of Life. Souls of Universal Consciousness in the Wisdom Sphere are in a position to do much to help the evolution of individual souls and consciousness in created reality. They come into possession of the divine ability to manifest themselves simultaneously in multiple forms of their choosing throughout created reality in all the Spheres on the Tree of Life. Hence, in their Universal Consciousness, they may manifest themselves, relate to and guide any number of individual souls at the same time. Most of this is probably done in the nine non-physical Spheres on the Tree of Life (e.g., through mental telepathy, dreams, visions, and other means); but there are exceptions to this. The well-known gospel accounts of Jesus' appearances in his "resurrection body," which he could shape, physically materialize, and dematerialize at will, are striking examples of such an exception.

In the Crown Sphere at the top of the Tree of Life (also called the "Thousand-Petalled Lotus" in Eastern Traditions), the Unconscious of individual human consciousness becomes Universal Cosmic Consciousness in the Limitless Light, Life, and Love of non-created Reality. This loving Universal Consciousness includes what we may call God's "divine microscope" that is focusing simultaneously through the true center of every individual soul and consciousness in created reality. Conversely, by allowing our individual consciousness to be drawn into the true center of our soul by the divine action in the gift of silent nonconceptual contemplation, we may eventually awaken into the non-dual universal pole of our being in God's Universal Consciousness.

From our limited perspectives of separate-self consciousness in the Personality/Astral Triad Spheres, we may only marvel at what divinely infused Universal Cosmic Consciousness, its capabilities, or the consciousness manifested in the resurrected and ascended Jesus may be. When Jesus ascended to Heaven in his resurrection body, his perfected individual consciousness ascended and transformed from the Spiritual/Moral Triad on the Tree of Life into the Universal Christ-Consciousness of the Supernal Triad and Limitless Light of non-created Reality. We're to follow him.

Appreciation and acknowledgement of such further reaches of evolving consciousness and the spiritual journey enlarge our perspective on created reality and God's Great Adventure. This awareness may serve to keep us humble where we currently are, and to prevent us from succumbing to temptations and delusions of ego-inflation and pride in the blessings and gifts we've received in the individual-consciousness Spheres of the Personality/Astral and Spiritual/Moral Triads—where all we have is what's given us by God and Higher Powers on the living Tree. We all have so much further to go and grow in the love of Christ and the goodness of God. As long as we're only an individual consciousness, we may, by God's grace, feel whole and complete in our true Self; but our spiritual journey into God is not fully complete. There's always more to discover and become!

9

THE WILL OF DIVINE LOVE

I

The Will of Divine Love is simple: We are utterly loved by God. God is within all of us and, with tender care and longing, God wants us to know God's presence and love deep in our hearts. This simple realization is the most wonderful discovery that holds the potential to free us from fear, sorrow, loneliness, and suffering—if we can integrate its implications and meaning into our consciousness and live true to it in human ground. Divine Love calls us to live free in the light of God's presence and love within us. I was briefly shown this sacred truth many years ago, in my mid-twenties, when something extraordinary happened that greatly enriched my life:

It was a spiritual initiation. By "initiation," I mean a new experience that inaugurates—but does not complete—a transition from one stage of being and consciousness into another. Spiritual initiations are important steps in our soul's evolutionary journey into God. There are minor and major initiations in a soul's spiritual journey. The experience that follows was, for me, a major spiritual initiation that I've been working to integrate into my personality, soul, and consciousness ever since it happened so many years ago.

Through a series of extraordinary experiences I couldn't explain, I'd gradually accepted and become aware that a higher evolved, nonphysical spiritual guide and teacher, who'd identified himself as *an old soul*, was inspiring at times and communicating with me from within—through dreams, intuitive insights, synchronous experiences, and a variety of meditative openings involving energy currents in my body and inner visions. On this particular occasion, I was meditating and focusing on the troubled human condition and the Bodhisattva ideal of love and compassion for humanity and all sentient beings. Suddenly, I felt a burst of subtle energy in the "third-eye" center of my forehead, which corresponds to the pituitary gland. My eyes were closed and I felt this energy center spinning like an expanding wheel that took me beyond the physical realm of the Kingdom Sphere into more subtle realms or Spheres of created reality.

I sensed an invisible presence carrying me through a vast expanse of inner space. We were traveling exceedingly fast over great distances. I noticed my eyes were blindfolded, so I could not see what was around me in any direction. Eventually, we landed on what seemed the top of a high mountain. My blindfold was removed. It was quiet and dark. The *old soul* who'd brought me here stepped aside and prostrated face-down before some invisible presence that was there. A current of lightning entered his head from above and his entire body lit up and glowed with a radiance of power, bliss, and love. I was awed and amazed to witness this.

After receiving this incredible anointing from an unseen Higher Power, the *old soul* got up and gestured me to do as he'd done. I stood where he'd stood and prostrated myself. At the same time, I was aware of my physical body sitting upright in meditation on a chair in a San Francisco apartment far below the place of this inner-space mountain top. Something touched the top of my head and an overwhelming current of lightning energy, bliss, and love streamed into me from above, filling my soul with a sacred, holy presence I'd never felt before. As this happened, I felt the holy energy streaming into my physical head and body where I sat in meditation. I was experiencing being in two different Spheres or planes of reality simultaneously. The incoming energy felt like it was too pure for me to tolerate as it rushed from my brain down my spine and into the suddenly supercharged psycho-spiritual energy centers of my human soul.

The unspeakable intensity of this new energy felt as if it may tear me apart, like a well-trained soprano voice shattering an empty crystal wine glass. I felt the awesome, third-person presence of God in this holy energy, which was at once humbling, exalting, and permeated with an astonishing sense of sacred eternity, divine immortality, and infinite love. It was too much for me to bear for more than a few timeless seconds. It was instantly obvious that I wasn't pure enough to tolerate this divine energy in my present state of psycho-spiritual development. I'd never imagined anything like this experience and what it suddenly revealed; and there was more to come.

After the dramatic sacred lightning bolt and overwhelming influx of its holy humbling energy impacting and changing forever the balance of psycho-spiritual energies in my soul, there came a sudden silent immersion of my consciousness into a most profound transcendent state of effortless serenity, peace, and caring preciousness. I was taken out of myself in a cloud of consciousness through the top of my head into an opening of intimate awesome encounter and communion with God in the second person; that is, with the presence of God as the divine beloved and lover of all souls. It seemed I went out from myself into this mysterious Great Cloud or silent bubble of indescribable peace and love that is somehow present and conscious in the true center of every soul in God's creation. I experienced a co-participation in part of the Divine Consciousness that abides in all souls and longs to give its Self, its love to every soul on Earth and beyond. Recalling this now, I'm reminded of Tielhard de Chardin's idea of the Planetary Noosphere (see chapter 3).

My outer prostration on this spiritual mountain top was accompanied by an inner prostration of the heart surrendering my separate-self will to God in a humble spirit of love, devotion, and dedication to the service of God's Divine Will or Plan for creation's perfection. God's incredibly gracious and surprising response to this surrender was to surrender back to me in loving humility with wordless generosity, kindness, and preciousness. This most intimate communion with God in the second person opens an inner door to spontaneously discovering the presence of God in the first person; that is, our identity or co-participation with God within us in the non-dual (without an opposite) oneness of Divine Love. This beginning movement of human consciousness into God's Divine Consciousness is simultaneously the individual soul's liberating fulfillment and a fulfillment of the Will of Divine Love; that is, God's fulfillment in the movement of

God's creation or work of art (individual soul) toward the completion of God's Divine Plan in us.

In receiving this profound contemplative gift of God's presence and action in the soul, we deeply experience as our own God's ardent longing that all souls may discover and know the goodness and love of the divine indwelling within them. This is the Will of Divine Love, and it becomes our own will and purpose to pursue in union with God. The blessed insight of God's Self-giving divine gesture and revelation of Divine Love in the soul as the root of intimacy with everything transcends the relative importance we pay to all lesser, dualistic perspectives. This awakening to Divine Love in the soul initiates a radically new perspective on reality. It reveals the ultimate good news, telling us for certain that everything is always all right and could never be otherwise, regardless of what happens or seems to happen in the drama and game of God's Great Adventure. This love-enlightened view of what is transcends created reality while including and integrating the dramatic opposites of shifting comedy and tragedy, of Good versus Evil into its universal perspective. This Divine Perspective is grounded in the unassailable serenity, perfection, and Will of Divine Love—the timeless Source, immutable essence, and spiritual inheritance of every evolving soul created in God.

II

After I got up from prostrating to the Divine Presence on the inner-plane mountain top, my blindfold was replaced and the *old soul* began flying me back across the Abyss separating this silent, sacred place of initiation from the Kingdom Sphere of physical reality and human life below. Silently we race through space above bottomless depths echoing a mysterious sound. Curiosity awakens: Why this blindfold? What's there to see? Raising my blindfold, I sneak a peek to find what's shown. Sudden shock assails my soul trembling in fear, panic, unbearable dread! In great cavern depths of chaos, I spy sinister black ring with glistening white eye in its center radiating a piercing power to draw me in.

Helpless terror chills my blood in ghastly vision of Severity Sphere forbidden me! In terrible timeless instant of shock and awe, I behold judgment hell in land of dead I dare not see. Separating power of wrath/reward ruling dual Universe of Good versus Evil casts grim, contrasting reflections utterly unlike bright perfection in non-dual Mercy Sphere of holy Love Above. I can't face this piercing gaze, judgment's lightning blaze shattering panicked maze in soul's glasshouse Tree. I'm exposed naked to the bone, feeling malignant all-seeing power pulling me in! Quickly, I pull my blindfold down to shut out horrors of hell threatening me!

This brief harrowing episode, and the earlier overwhelming intensity of my initiation experience, made me acutely aware of my need for inner purification and healing. In retrospect, I now see that I was shown a stark contrast between the Spheres of Severity and Mercy on the Qabalistic Tree of Life. The *old soul* who took me there is, I believe, a highly evolved Master of Compassion residing in the Mercy Sphere of non-dual Divine Love. A knight of right in the armor of love, the *old soul* commands the powers of Severity's fearsome realms because he, unlike me, has passed through the judgment of righteousness (the spiritual test of Severity) and has become one with the Will of Divine Love. Hence, he could protect and carry me over the Abyss of Judgment's terror and bring me safely to Higher Ground on the mountain peak of initiation in the Sphere of Mercy.

Beyond the integral stages of individual consciousness evolution, which reach their climax in the non-dual Mercy Sphere, there comes the evolution of individual souls into the fields of Universal Consciousness in the Tree's Supernal Triad and Limitless Light of non-created Reality. The Higher Power to which the *old soul* and I prostrated is, I believe, the Universal Consciousness of the Wisdom Sphere of God the Father, which is directly above the Mercy Sphere on the Tree (see diagram on page 7). Our contact with this Supernal-Triad Sphere was mediated by a holy Hierophant Being functioning in service to the Will of Divine Love. This unseen Higher Being brought the Higher Energies of Initiation down into us from the Supernal-Wisdom Sphere of God the Father through what's called in esoteric literature "the Rod of Initiation."[1]

The implications of the above spiritual initiation experience are profound and far-reaching. It gave me a new sense of direction based on a vivid glimpse of spiritual territory far in advance of where I was grounded in my soul's spiritual journey. This precious, enlightening glimpse was not a permanent transformation of my soul and consciousness into Divine Consciousness but rather the beginning of a work that has, at least in my case, required a lifetime of subsequent effort and is still in process. It confirmed for me like nothing else could how infinitely real, good, loving, and mighty God is, how we are all part of God and how God is part (the best part) of each of us. Through a brief partial participation in the Universal Consciousness of Divine Love, I was given to know that it is the Will of Divine Love for all souls to know this.

The Will of Divine Love wants every soul to know it is loved and not separate. This is the silent imperative of yearning in the deep heart of God, and in the unconscious true center (Sphere of Christ/Beauty) in every soul. The gift of nonconceptual contemplation, into which Centering Prayer leads us, is the holy inner process that brings this yearning to fulfillment. Through the inner work of this process—carried on with our consent and cooperation by the divine action in us—we gradually learn to live under will and guidance from Above. This is a core lesson of the spiritual journey. By "Above," we mean the Spiritual/Moral and Supernal Triads of the soul's Tree of Life, where microcosm and Macrocosm are united in Divine Love.

We live in God and are loved through and through, perfectly and completely by God. In my initiation experience, I felt how God longs for each soul to know this and sensed that we may all serve God's Will, the Will of Divine Love, by doing all we can to open and awaken to God's presence in us, and to humbly encourage and lovingly support this spiritual awakening in others and the world at large. Thomas Keating has said that to do the will of another is, in a very real sense, to become one with that other. As our union of wills with God grows, so does our spiritual union with God and the Will of Divine Love grow and evolve until we are fully transformed into Christ. The consent of Centering Prayer—to God's presence and action in us—starts and continues us on this journey.

Perhaps the Will of Divine Love reveals, to whatever degree we may grasp it, the psychology of God in terms of God's motivation in manifesting created reality within the holy Spheres of the Divine Consciousness? Divine Love is the foundation of and key to Spiritual Psychology in all souls and throughout God's creation. In other words, non-created Reality is the origin, ending, and Source of all energies, possibilities, and Laws manifesting and governing created reality. What this all ultimately boils down to in the great alchemical caldron of consciousness, chaos, and order is the invincible Will of Divine Love that makes *everything* ultimately all right.

The reassuring message of Divine Love's presence in all souls is that no matter what may happen in any version of God's Great Adventure, everything will always be all right and could not possibly be otherwise. The ultimate truth and reality of non-created, non-dual eternal Divine Love overrules the considerations and judgments of all lesser, egocentric perspectives that may arise in created reality. Love *is* Truth. It is the core truth of every soul created in the divine image and likeness. The spiritual tragedy of the human condition is that we fail to realize this liberating truth of love and its amazingly wonderful implications.

Again, it became unquestionably clear to me in the above spiritual-initiation experience that the Will of Divine Love is for *all* souls to know the truth of God's presence in and great love for each of us, no matter who we are or what mistakes we've made as individual actors in the drama and game of God's Great Adventure. I saw intuitively for myself how the Divine Presence is fully present to everyone all the time. This core spiritual insight, combined with some partial participation in God's longing desire that all souls may consciously share in God's loving presence in us, gives us a most meaningful purpose to serve in human life and beyond.

We are invited or called by God to serve this divine purpose—the Will of Divine Love—by working to further our spiritual growth in love and to serve this growth in others in whatever ways we can. These are the greatest contributions we may make toward the fulfillment of our highest human destiny and the evolution of our Planetary Noosphere.

As Love determines Justice, so does Will determine Destiny. We come from Divine Love and our destiny, as individual souls, is to consciously evolve into and become the Divine Love that we, in truth, already are. We have but to grow in and choose love, and to unite our will to that of Divine Love. Love reverses entropy and evolves consciousness throughout created reality. It is the Source of each soul's immortality.

NOTES

1. GOD'S GREAT ADVENTURE, PART ONE

1. "To be or not to be, that is the question?" These are the famous words of William Shakespeare's character, Hamlet, in the play of the same name.

2. I discuss Integral Theory in *The One Who Loves Us: Centering Prayer and Evolving Consciousness*. Integral Theory's basic stages of consciousness evolution are: the *tribal, warrior, traditional, modern, postmodern, and integral* stages. Also, for more details, see *Integral Christianity* by Paul Smith and *Integral Spirituality* by Ken Wilber. For more on the Tree of Life, see *The Hermetic Qabalah & the Tree of Life* by Paul A. Clark; *A Practical Guide To Qabalistic Symbolism* by Gareth Knight; and *The Mystical Qabalah* by Dion Fortune.

3. A fuller, more detailed description of the Tree is given in my book, *Centering Prayer and Rebirth in Christ on the Tree of Life: the process of inner transformation*.

4. The stages of evolving consciousness and grades of evolving love (bronze, silver, and gold) are discussed in *The One Who Loves* Us. For more on the Zero Point Field, see *Centering Prayer and Rebirth in Christ on the Tree of Life*, pp. 57–61. Also, see *The Field* by Lynne McTaggert.

5. Hear: Rev. Ann Davies, "Tree of Life Series," CD # 1.

6. This process of inner transformation is discussed in detail and depth in my book, *Centering Prayer and Rebirth in Christ on the Tree of Life*.

2. GOD'S GREAT ADVENTURE, PART TWO

1. I discuss Integral Theory in relation to twentieth-first-century interpretations of Christianity in *The One Who Loves Us: Centering Prayer and Evolving Consciousness* (chapters 4 and 5). Also see *Integral Christianity* by Paul Smith, and Ken Wilber's books: *The Integral Vision, Integral Psychology,* and *Integral Spirituality.*

2. See, for example, Thomas Keating's books: *The Mystery of Christ; Intimacy with God;* and *The Human Condition;* also my book, *Human Ground, Spiritual Ground: Paradise Lost and Found.*

3. The multilayered Collective Unconscious—shared by all humans—underlies our personal unconscious and is said to contain, among other things, the evolutionary history, experiential imprints, living symbols (archetypes), images and collective memory of all humanity and life on Earth. For more information, see: Jung's *The Archetypes and the Collective*

Unconscious; The Origins and History of Consciousness by Erich Neumann; and *Archetypes: A Natural History of the Self* by Anthony Stevens.

4. I've written about this in more detail in *Human Ground, Spiritual Ground.* See especially chapters 11, "Identity Quest and Cultural Conditioning," and 12, "Cultural Conditioning and Identity Shift."

5. For more details regarding the Renaissance, Enlightenment, and origins of modern-stage consciousness, see my book, *The One Who Loves Us: Centering Prayer and Evolving Consciousness*, chapter 5; and see *Spontaneous Evolution* by Bruce Lipton and Steve Baherman.

6. The details of how evolving consciousness shapes individual and group interpretations of religion and spirituality are discussed in Paul Smith's book, *Integral Christianity: the Spirit's call to evolve*; and in my *The One Who Loves Us.*

7. "Scientism" is the extreme modernist belief that truth is exclusively objective and may be known only via scientifically verified experiments that may be controlled and repeated.

8. Prof. Robert Soloman, in his video course, "No Excuses: Existentialism and the Meaning of Life," describes the philosophy of postmodernism (also called "poststructuralism"), as sometimes rejecting the ideas of rationality, objectivity, truth, and knowledge, as well as "the idea of a unified self and the clarifying powers of reason."

9. This is described in detail in *Centering Prayer and Rebirth in Christ on the Tree of Life;* see chapter 12.

10. The "micro-spirituality" of evolving human souls includes the full spectrum of positive, negative, and neutral attitudes that may motivate our behavior, ranging from the best to the worst. In contrast to the micro-spirituality of evolving souls is the Macro-Spirituality and Divine Love of God or non-created Reality, which does not evolve because it already is perfect and complete. The micro-spirituality of individual souls evolves to ultimately become one with the Macro-Spirituality of God. This is the Will of Divine Love. I introduce and discuss micro-spirituality and Macro-Spirituality in Chapter One of *The One Who Loves Us.*

3. GOD'S GREAT ADVENTURE, PART THREE

1. In addition to *Man's Place in Nature*, de Chardin's books *The Phenomenon of Man* and *The Future of Man* present his modern, scientific ideas about planetary evolution and consciousness in clear detail.

2. De Chardin discusses the idea of intelligent life on other, distant planets and the scientific basis of this probability in his article, "A Sequel to the Problem of Human Origins: The Plurality of Inhabited Worlds," in *Christianity and Evolution: Reflections on Science and Religion.*

3. In addition to such seemingly random cosmic events affecting the evolution of life on Earth, we may not, with certainty, rule out the possibility of more conscious and deliberate interventions by higher evolved extraterrestrial species (physical or non-physical)—as has been suggested by such writers as Immanuel Velikofsky (*Worlds in Collision*); Zachariah Sitchin (*Genesis Revisited*), and Erich von Daniken (*Chariots of the Gods*).

4. *Man's Place in Nature*, p. 62.

5. Ibid., p. 76.

6. The false-self system is described in Thomas Keatings books: *The Human Condition*; *Invitation to Love*; and *The Mystery of Christ*. My book, *Human Ground, Spiritual Ground*, builds on Fr. Keating's work, discussing the four universal parameters of human existence, our basic instinctual needs in their healthy expressions as well as their distortions into pathological emotional happiness programs.

7. This possibility is suggested by various phenomena of group consciousness among humans and primates, such as that suggested in the book, *The Hundredth Monkey*. In this case, a young monkey on an island off the coast of Japan began washing its sweet potatoes (provided by experimenters who dropped them in the sand) in the ocean to clean them off before eating them. Other monkeys on the same island, seeing the monkey do this, began to do the same thing over a period of years. Once a certain critical number of monkeys (suppose it's 100) on this first island had begun washing their sandy sweet potatoes in the ocean before eating them, all the monkeys on the surrounding islands and on the mainland spontaneously began doing the same thing.

    The monkeys on these separate islands and on the mainland had no physical contact with one another. The idea that the monkeys in surrounding isolated areas reportedly *all* made this transition into a new behavior pattern simultaneously suggests that a non-physical, psychic, or noospheric type of influence was involved. Using this "hundredth-monkey" idea, we may suggest that a certain, unknown number of humans evolving toward de Chardin's Omega Point in harmony with the Will of Divine Love, could produce the "hundredth-monkey effect" on a spiritual level and radically impact the attitudes and consciousness of the entire human species in a most positive and beneficial way. Hence, each of us working on our own spiritual growth is a great service to all humanity.

4. GOOD VERSUS EVIL

1. *Eros* and *Thanatos* are mythological Greek gods representing the forces of life and death respectively.

2. The spiritual principles of "Good and Evil" are introduced in Genesis 1:17 and 3:1–7 when the character of the Lord God warns Adam not to eat the forbidden fruit on "the tree of the knowledge of good and evil," and when Adam and Eve, encouraged by the talking Serpent (who embodies creation's instinctual life-force energy), do eat it and "the eyes of both were opened."

In *The Avesta* of Zoroastrianism, the pre-Christian religion of ancient Persia, Ahura Mazda and Ahriman personify the principles of Good versus Evil respectively. In Hinduism, Queen Maya and her minions represent the alluring forces of illusion and Evil while the avatars of Vishnu (e.g., Rama, Krishna, and Kalki) personify the forces of truth, righteousness, and the Good. In Buddhism, Mara is known as "the evil one" who enslaves sentient beings into the bondage of ignorance and suffering while the Buddha, "the fully enlightened one," guides unenlightened beings along "the Noble Eightfold Path" leading to Liberation and Enlightenment. In Islam, which recognizes the books of the Old and New Testaments as well as the Holy Quran as sacred, the principles of Good and Evil are associated with the Fall of Adam, forgetfulness of the one true God (Allah), the greater *jihad* (struggle between Good and Evil within the individual soul) which, when successful, leads to the conscious remembrance of Allah together with faithfulness to His divine Will and Laws (see *The Islamic Tradition: An Introduction* by Victor Danner).

3. See, for example, Elaine Pagels's *The Origin of Satan* for a detailed description of the historical/social development of the idea of Satan, first as an angel of God (doing God's Will) and later as a personification of the principle of Evil in the Judeo-Christian Tradition. Also see "The War of the Sons of Light and the Sons of Darkness" in *The Dead Sea Scriptures*, T. H. Gaster, translator.

4. This figure of 10,000 years is according to the Integral Theory of evolving consciousness. See *Integral Christianity* by Paul Smith.

5. For more regarding the nature of Good/Evil and their tendencies toward affirmation or negation of life, existence, and consciousness, see my books: *Human Ground, Spiritual Ground* (chapter 4 "Good/Evil in Human Ground"); and *Centering Prayer and Rebirth in Christ on the Tree of Life* (chapter 6 "Malkuth/Kingdom and Daath/the Cloud).

6. To create, the absolutely non-dual consciousness of non-created Reality has to manifest duality within itself, establishing the separation of two complementary poles (positive and negative or masculine and feminine poles) so that there may be a dynamic energy flow between them to generate created reality with the images and possibilities it manifests. See the description of the Qabalistic Tree of Life in Chapter One of this book and, for more detail, Chapter Three in *Centering Prayer and Rebirth in Christ on the Tree of Life*.

7. The false self's motivational agendas or emotional happiness programs are described in detail in my book, *Human Ground, Spiritual Ground: Paradise Lost and Found—A reflection on Centering Prayer's Conceptual Background*. Also see Thomas Keating's books: *The Mystery of Christ*; *Invitation to Love*; *Intimacy with God*; and *The Human Condition*.

8. These atheistic attitudes, materialistic views of reality and abuses of Nature are expressed in the nihilistic philosophy of negative postmodernism, in Darwin's "survival of the fittest" theory, the writings of Sigmund Freud, and elsewhere. See, for example, *Spontaneous Evolution* by Bruce

Lipton and Steven Baherman, *The Art of War* by Sun Tzu, *The Prince* by Michaelvelli, and *Whale Walker's Morning* by poet Michael Shorb.

9. I read these quoted words many years ago in the book, *The Sacred Tarot* by C. C. Zain (Elbert Benjamin), pp. 82–83. They are attributed by him to an ancient Egyptian Mystery School. This text reads further: "Every will that lets itself be governed by the instincts of the flesh abdicates its liberty and is bound to the expiation of its errors. On the contrary, every will which unites itself to Deity, in order to manifest Truth and work Justice, enters, even in this life, into a participation of Divine Power over beings and things." Here we have an example of the archetypal Good/Evil conflict expressed in a text attributed to an ancient Western Mystery School.

10. Our basic instinctual needs are described in detail in my book: *Human Ground, Spiritual Ground.*

11. See *The Marriage of Heaven and Hell* by William Blake.

5. CENTERING PRAYER AND SPIRITUAL PSYCHOLOGY

1. Thomas Keating's books, *Open Mind, Open Heart* and *Intimacy with God*; Carl Arico's *A Taste of Silence*; David Muyskens' *Forty Days to a Closer Walk with God*; Murchadh O' Madagain's *Centering Prayer and the Healing of the Unconscious*; David Frenette's *The Path of Centering Prayer*; and Peter Traben Haas' *A Beautiful Prayer: Answering Common Misperceptions about Centering Prayer*, are fine examples of books on the method of Centering Prayer that include some of the practical workings of Spiritual Psychology.

2. *The Art of Loving* by Eric Fromm, pp. 7–36.

3. Macro-spirituality and micro-spirituality are described in detail in *The One Who Loves Us*, Chapter One: "What is Spirituality?"

4. These needs are discussed in detail in *Human Ground, Spiritual Ground.*

5. Transpersonal Psychology: Carl Jung, Abraham Maslow, and Roberto Assagioli are prominent among the founders and pioneers of Transpersonal Psychology.

6. In John 15:5–6, Jesus says: "I am the vine, you are the branches. Those who abide in me and I in them bear much fruit, because apart from me you can do nothing. Whoever does not abide in me is thrown away like a branch and withers; such branches are gathered, thrown into the fire, and burned." This destroying "fire" Jesus mentions corresponds to the dark, disintegrating abyss of the Qlippoth beneath the Tree of Life.

7. See *The Future of Man*, pp. 270–312.

8. See *Frankenstein* by Mary Shelly and the film versions of this 19th Century classic novel.

9. *Invitation to Love*, p. 37.

10. I first encountered the "no-exit" situation ("no way out in time or space") as expressing the archetype of hell in Stanislav Grof's pioneering work, *Realms of the Human Unconscious*.

11. See *Invitation to Love, Intimacy with God* and *Divine Therapy & Addiction* by Thomas Keating.

12. See *The Collected Works of St. John of the Cross*, Teresa of Avila's *The Interior Castle*, *Integral Christianity* by Paul Smith, *Integral Spirituality* by Ken Wilber, and Centering Prayer's conceptual background. For detailed information about Centering Prayer's conceptual background, see Thomas Keating's previously mentioned books and his video talks, "The Psychological Experience of Centering Prayer," "The Fruits and Gifts of the Spirit," and "Heartfulness: Transformation in Christ." Also, see *Human Ground, Spiritual Ground*.

13. These three non-physical Walls of deepening conscious experience are introduced in my book, *Centering Prayer and Rebirth in Christ on the Tree of Life*, pp. 136–138.

14. See *The Subtle Body: An Encyclopedia of Your Energetic Anatomy* by Cyndi Dale for a detailed multi-traditional presentation of the Wall of Energy in the human soul.

15. Thomas Keating discusses "lights-on" and "lights-off" mysticism in "The Spiritual Journey" series, talks 18 (Night of Sense) and 19 (Night of Spirit) where he compares the "exuberant mysticism" of Teresa of Avila with the "hidden ladder" of John of the Cross. I also discuss these two modes of spiritual experience in *Centering Prayer and Rebirth in Christ on the Tree of Life*, pp. 128–129; 140–142.

16. See *Centering Prayer and Rebirth in Christ on the Tree of Life*, chapter 11: "The Mystery of Daath/the Cloud."

17. See *The Ascent of Mount Carmel* and *The Dark Night* in *The Collected Works of St. John of the Cross*; also, *The Dark Night of the Soul: A Psychiatrist Explores the Connection Between Darkness and Spiritual Growth* by Gerald G. May.

6. THE TRANSCENDENT FUNCTION

1. See chapter 5, "Sigmund Freud," in Jung's autobiography, *Memories, Dreams, Reflections*.

2. *Ibid*, see chapter 6, "Confrontation with the Unconscious."

3. See *Imago Dei* in *The Archetypes and the Collective Unconscious* and in *Aion: Researches into the Phenomenology of the Self* (Collected Works, vol. 9, parts I and II). In *Aion*, Jung's thesis is that, for the Western psyche, the figure of Christ is the most appropriate symbol of the Self or central archetype of psychic wholeness.

4. See "The Transcendent Function," in *The Structure and Dynamics of the Psyche* (Collected Works, vol. 8). The Transcendent Function is mentioned

in many of Jung's Collected Works and in his biographies by Marie-Louise von Franz and Deirdre Bair.

5. See Thomas Keating's *The Human Condition*, pp. 18–19.

6. See "The Unloading of The Unconscious" in Thomas Keating's *Open Mind, Open Heart*.

7. *The Red Book*, p. VII.

8. Some additional reasons are given by Ulrick Hoernt in his preface to the *Red Book*.

9. C. G. Jung and Gerhard Adler, *The Structure and Dynamics of the Psyche*, pp. 67–91.

10. See Thomas Keating's previously mentioned books and my *Human Ground, Spiritual Ground*.

11. *The Structure and Dynamics of the Psyche*, pp. 78–79.

12. Ibid., p. 68.

13. Marie-Luise von Franz, *C. G. Jung: His Myth in Our Time*, p. 111.

14. Ibid., pp. 99–253; Also see: *Memories, Dreams, Reflections*; *C. G. Jung: Word and Image*; and, for full depth, Jung's Collected Works, vol. 11 *Psychology and Religion: West and East*; Vol. 12 *Psychology and Alchemy*, vol. 13, *Alchemical Studies*; and vol. 14, *Mysterium Coniunctionis*.

15. Marie-Luise von Franz, *C. G. Jung: His Myth in Our Time*, pp. 111–112.

16. Collected Works, vol. 18, *The Symbolic Life*, pp. 690–691.

7. WORKING WITH THE UNCONSCIOUS

1. For more examples and information on this topic, see "The Active Prayer Sentence," appendix 2 in *Open Mind, Open Heart* by Thomas Keating, pp. 171–72; and the Contemplative Life Program Praxis, *Active Prayer: Pray without Ceasing*, published by Contemplative Outreach.

2. For detailed discussion and descriptions of the false self and its happiness programs, see *Human Ground, Spiritual Ground* and Thomas Keating's previously mentioned works.

3. The way of the Cross is discussed in *The One Who Loves Us*. See chapters 3, "Through a Mystical Christian Window," and 5, "Prayer is Relating to God."

4. See *Centering Prayer and Rebirth in Christ on the Tree of Life*, chapter 9, "Personality Patterns on the Tree of Life," pp. 112–118, for discussion of personal habits as living, conscious entities in the soul.

5. See *Addiction and Grace* by Gerald May and *The Body Keeps the Score: Brain, Mind, and Body in the Healing of Trauma* by Bessel Van Der Klok, M.D.

6. Welcoming Prayer brochure, available from Contemplative Outreach.

7. For full details regarding practicing the Welcoming Prayer, see the beautifully written Contemplative Life Program praxis: *Welcoming Prayer: Consent on the Go.*

8. Fr. Carl Arico pointed this important fact out to me some years ago.

9. See the Contemplative Life Program praxis, *Forgiveness*, and the related CD, "The Forgiveness Prayer Process," with Fr. Carl Arico.

10. See: Kathleen Dowling Singh, *The Grace in Dying*, pp. 167–168; and Elisabeth Kübler-Ross, *On Death and Dying.*

11. See "Proverbs of Hell" (I).

12. The idea of psychological concepts "impoverishing life" is suggested by Jungian psychologist James Hillman in *Lament of the Dead: Psychology after Jung's Red Book*, p. 204.

13. Paul taught his "Just Noticing" practice at Holy Spirit Center in Anchorage, Alaska during silent Centering Prayer retreats in Aug. 2012 and Jan. 2014.

14. These quotes are from the flyer for one of Paul Ilecki's "Just Noticing" retreat workshops at St. Benedict's Monastery Retreat House in Snowmass, Colorado.

8. SOME FURTHER REACHES OF EVOLVING CONSCIOUSNESS

1. "Daath/the Cloud" is discussed in detail in my *Centering Prayer and Rebirth in Christ on the Tree of Life.*

2. Ibid., see Chapter Seven, "Our Divine Inheritance," for a fuller description of the individual soul's origins and its journey down the Tree of Life into physical incarnation.

9. THE WILL OF DIVINE LOVE

1. The energy path running between the Mercy Sphere and the Wisdom Sphere on the Tree of Life is represented in Tarot by Major Arcanum Five, The Hierophant—who gives initiation into the Sacred Mysteries. See *The Tarot: A Key to the Wisdom of the Ages* by Paul Foster Case. The soul's major initiations and "the Rod of Initiation" are explained in Alice Bailey's classic work: *Initiation, Human and Solar* (first published in 1922). Also, see Haroutiun Saraydarian's: *Christ the Avatar of Sacrificial Love*, regarding Esoteric Christianity and for descriptions of the soul's major spiritual initiations in terms of major events in the life and story of Jesus.

REFERENCES

Anon. *A Course in Miracles*. Glen Ellen, CA: Foundation for Inner Peace, 1985.

Arico, C. *A Taste of Silence*. New York: Lantern, 2015.

Assagioli, R. *Psychosynthesis*. New York: Viking, 1965.

Bailey, A. *Initiation, Human and Solar*. New York: Lucis Publishing, 1992.

Bair, D. *Jung: A Biography*. New York: Little, Brown, 2003.

Blake, W. *The Marriage of Heaven and Hell*. Oxford: Benediction Classics, 2010.

Case, P. F. *The Tarot: A Key to the Wisdom of the Ages*. New York: Tarcher, 2006.

Chodorow, J. (ed.). *Jung on Active Imagination*. Princeton, NJ: Princeton Univ. Press, 1997.

Clark, P. *The Hermetic Qabalah and the Tree of Life*. Covina, CA: Fraternity of the Hidden Light, 2012.

Contemplative Life Program. *Active Prayer*. Butler, NJ: Contemplative Outreach, 2005.

———. *Forgiveness*. Butler, NJ: Contemplative Outreach, 2005.

———. *Welcoming Prayer: Consent on the Go*. Butler, NJ: Contemplative Outreach, 2014.

Dale, C. *The Subtle Body*. Boulder, CO: Sounds True, 2009.

Danner, V. *The Islamic Tradition*. New York: Amity House, 1988.

de Chardin, P. T. *Christianity and Evolution*. New York: Harcourt, 1971.

———. *The Divine Milieu*. New York: Harper, 2001.

———. *The Future of Man*. New York: Doubleday, 1964.

———. *Man's Place in Nature*. New York: Harper and Row, 1966.

———. *The Phenomenon of Man*. New York: Harper, 1975.

Delio, I. (ed.). *From Tielhard to Omega*. Maryknoll, NY: Orbis, 2014.

Dowling-Singh, K. *The Grace in Dying*. San Francisco: HarperCollins, 1998.

Dupre, L. and J. Wiseman (ed.). *Light from Light: An Anthology of Christian Mysticism*. New York: Paulist Press, 1988.

Fortune, D. *The Mystical Qabalah*. Boston: Weiser, 2000.

Frenette, D. *The Path of Centering Prayer*. Boulder, CO: Sounds True, 2012.

Freud, S. *Beyond the Pleasure Principle*. New York: Liveright, 1961.

Frey, K. *Centering Prayer and Rebirth in Christ on the Tree of Life*. Great Barrington, MA: Portal Books, 2013.

————. *Human Ground, Spiritual Ground*. Great Barrington, MA: Portal Books, 2012.

————. *The One Who Loves Us*. Great Barrington, MA: Portal Books, 2014.

Fromm, E. *The Art of Loving*. New York: Harper, 2006.

Gaster, T. (tr.). *The Dead Sea Scriptures*. New York: Anchor, 1976.

Grof, S. *Realms of the Human Unconscious*. New York: Dutton, 1976.

Hillman, J. and S. Shamdasani. *Lament of the Dead: Psychology after Jung's Red Book*. New York: W.W. Norton, 2013.

Holy Bible: NRSV. New York: Oxford Univ. Press, 1989.

John of the Cross, Saint. *The Collected Works of St. John of the Cross* (tr. K. Kavanaugh and O. Rodriguez). Washington, DC: ICS, 1979.

Jung, C. G. *The Collected Works of C. G. Jung*. Princeton: Bollingen Series XX, Princeton Univ.:

————. *Aion: Researches into the Phenomenology of the Self*, vol. 9, part 2, 1979.

————. *Alchemical Studies*, vol. 13, 1983.

————. *The Archetypes and the Collective Unconscious*, vol. 9, part 1, 1980.

————. *C. G. Jung: Word and Image*. Princeton, NJ: Princeton Univ., 1979.

————. *Memories, Dreams, Reflections*. New York: Vintage, 1965.

————. *Mysterium Coniunctionis*, vol. 14, 1977.

————. *Psychology and Alchemy*, vol. 12, New York: Pantheon, 1953.

————. *Psychology and Religion: West and East*, vol. 11, 1977.

————. *The Red Book: Liber Novus*. New York: Norton, 2009.

————. *The Structure and Dynamics of the Psyche*, vol. 8, 1969.

————. *The Symbolic Life*, vol. 18, 1980.

Keating, T. *Divine Therapy & Addiction*. New York: Lantern, 2009.

————. *The Human Condition*. New York: Paulist, 1999.

————. *Invitation to Love*. New York: Continuum, 1992.

————. *Intimacy with God*. New York: Crossroad, 2009.

————. *The Mystery of Christ*. New York: Continuum, 2003.

————. *Open Mind, Open Heart*. New York: Continuum, 2006.

Keyes, K. *The Hundredth Monkey*. Coos Bay, OR: Vision Books, 1982.

Knight, G. *A Practical Guide to Qabalistic Symbolism*. Boston: Weiser, 2001.

Kübler-Ross, E. *On Death and Dying*. New York: Macmillan, 1969.

Lipton, B., and S. Baherman. *Spontaneous Evolution*. Carlsbad, CA: Hay House, 2009.

Maslow, A. *Toward a Psychology of Being*. New York: Van Nostrand Reinhold, 1968.

May, G. *Addiction and Grace*. San Francisco: Harper, 1991.

———. *The Dark Night of the Soul*. San Francisco: Harper, 2004.

McTaggert, L. *The Field*. New York: Harper, 2008.

Meninger. W. *Julian of Norwich: a Mystic for Today*. Great Barrington, MA: Lindisfarne Books, 2010.

———. *The Process of Forgiveness*. New York: Continuum, 1996.

Machiavelli, N. *The Prince*. New York: Penguin, 1999.

Myskens, D. *Forty Days to a Closer Walk with God*. Nashville, TN: Upper Room, 2006.

Neumann, E. *The Origins and History of Consciousness*. Princeton, NJ: Princeton Univ. Press, 1971.

The New American Bible. New York: Catholic Publishing, 1991.

The New Jerusalem Bible. New York: Doubleday, 1985.

Ó Madagáin, M. *Centering Prayer and the Healing of the Unconscious*. New York: Lantern, 2007.

Pagels, E. *The Origin of Satan*. New York: Vintage Books, 1995.

Saraydarian, H. *Christ: The Avatar of Sacrificial Love*. Sedona, AZ: Aquarian Educational Group, 1974.

Shelly, M. *Frankenstein: A Modern Prometheus*. New York: Penguin, 2003.

Shorb, M. *Whale Walker's Morning: New and Selected Poems*. Pasadena, CA: Shabda Press, 2013.

Sitchin, Z. *Genesis Revisited*. New York: Avon Books, 1990.

Smith, P. *Integral Christianity*. St. Paul, MN: Paragon House, 2011.

Stevens, A. *Archetypes: A Natural History of the Self*. New York: Quill, 1983.

Teresa of Avila, Saint. *The Interior Castle* (tr. K. Kavanaugh and O. Rodriguez). Mahwah, NJ: Paulist Press, 1979.

Traben Hass, P. *A Beautiful Prayer*. Austin, TX: Contemplative Christians, 2014.

Tzu, S. (tr. Thomas Cleary). *The Art of War*. Boston: Shambalah, 2005.

Van Der Klok, B. *The Body Keeps the Score*. New York: Viking, 2014.

Velikovsky, I. *Worlds in Collision*. New York: Doubleday, 1950.

Von Daniken, E. *Chariots of the Gods*. New York: Berkley Books, 1999.

von Franz, M. L. *C. G. Alchemical Active Imagination*. Boston: Shambhala, 1997.

———. *Jung: His Myth in Our Time*. Boston: Little, Brown, 1975.

Wilber, K. *Integral Psychology*. Boston: Shambalah, 2000.

———. *Integral Spiriuality*. Boston: Integral Books, 2006.

———. *The Integral Vision*. Boston: Shambalah, 2007.

Zain, C. C. *The Sacred Tarot*. Los Angeles: The Church of Light, 2005.

OTHER REFERENCES

Audio:

Fr. Carl Arico: "The Forgiveness Prayer Process." Contemplative Outreach Store: ph. 1-800-608-0096 or www.contemplativeoutreach.org.

Rev. Ann Davies: "Tree of Life" Series. Builders of the Adytum: ph: 1-323-255-7141 or www.bota.org.

Video:

Thomas Keating: Spiritual Journey Series: #18 "The Night of Sense" and #19 "The Night of Spirit," "The Psychological Experience of Centering Prayer," and "Heartfulness: Transformation in Christ," with Betty Sue Flowers. Contemplative Outreach Store.

Prof. Robert Soloman: "No Excuses: Existentialism and the Meaning of Life." The Teaching Company: ph. 1-800-832-2412 or www.TEACH12.com.

CONTEMPLATIVE OUTREACH is a spiritual network of individuals and small faith communities committed to living the contemplative dimension of the Gospel. The common desire for Divine transformation, primarily expressed through a commitment to a daily Centering Prayer practice, unites our international, interdenominational community.

Today, Contemplative Outreach annually serves over 40,000 people; supports more than 120 active contemplative chapters in 39 countries; supports more than 800 prayer groups; teaches more than 15,000 people the practice of Centering Prayer and other contemplative practices through locally hosted workshops; and provides training and resources to local chapters and volunteers. We also publish and distribute the wisdom teachings of Fr. Thomas Keating and other resources that support the contemplative life.

Contemplative Outreach, Ltd.
10 Park Place, 2nd Floor, Suite B
Butler, New Jersey 07405

973-838-3384
Fax 973-492-5795
Email: office@coutreach.org
www.contemplativeoutreach.org

KESS FREY was born in 1945 and grew up in the Eagle Rock neighborhood of North Los Angeles. In 1968, he graduated in Psychology at the University of California, Irvine. He has studied Eastern and Western philosophy, psychology, and religion since 1965, with particular interests in meditation and depth psychology. He was raised Catholic and is a Catholic Christian who honors the contemplative dimension of all religions and spiritual paths. His principal spiritual teachers have been Lama Anagarika Govinda (German), Chogyam Trungpa, Rinpoche (Tibetan), Swami Amar Jyoti (East Indian), and, since 1989, Fr. Thomas Keating (American).

Mr. Frey has lived in Anchorage, Alaska since 1983, where he worked with school-age children for twenty years. He has been involved with Centering Prayer since 1989, is affiliated with Contemplative Outreach, Ltd., and offers introductory Centering Prayer workshops, facilitates prayer groups and silent retreats, and is active in prison ministry. He is the author of five previous books: *Satsang Notes of Swami Amar Jyoti* (1977); *The Creation of Reality* (1986); *Human Ground, Spiritual Ground: Paradise Lost and Found: A Reflection on Centering Prayer's Conceptual Background* (2012); *Centering Prayer and Rebirth in Christ on the Tree of Life: The Process of Inner Transformation* (2013); and most recently, *The One Who Loves Us: Centering Prayer and Evolving Consciousness* (2014).